DELIVERING AND MANAGING EFFECTIVE RE IN THE SECONDARY SCHOOL

Chris Wright & Isobel Vale

Courseware Publications

1997

INDEX OF CONTENTS

Section 1.
A BRIEF HISTORY

Religious Instruction shall be given in every county school and in every voluntary school.

1944 Education Act Section 25.2.

It is the intention of the Government and of the Bill that the religious instruction required to be given shall be Christian instruction, and that the corporate act of worship shall be an act of Christian worship.

Parliamentary Debates, Hansard 4th series, 132,366.

The teaching of RE 'shall reflect the fact that the religious traditions in Great Britain are in the main Christian whilst taking account of the teaching and practices of the other principal religions represented in Great Britain.

Education Reform Act, 1988, Section 7.

1870 - 1944	

The first schools in Great Britain were provided by religious institutions. In these schools, the religious instruction provided largely consisted of instruction into the faith. Religious instruction and school worship had similar aims. In 1870, Forster's Education Act included religious instruction as part of the curriculum for Board Schools. The aim of such education was to teach children how to be Christian. Since many of the schools were attached to a particular denomination, such teaching was seen as one way of gaining members for the church. The Liberal MP, W. Cowper-Temple moved for an amendment to this act which became known as the Cowper-Temple clause. It said that, in the newly established Board Schools, 'no religious catechism or formulary distinctive of any particular denomination shall be taught'.

In the 1920s, there was a significant change in the nature of the syllabuses. Instead of being lists of things to memorise, an attempt was made to introduce theological aims. Religious instruction and school worship became opportunities for nurturing. For example, the stated aim of the *Winchester Syllabus* (1921) was, 'to give instruction in the Christian faith as a living thing, with power over daily life'. The *Cambridgeshire Syllabus* (1924) saw the school as a Christian community with a responsibility to nurture pupils in the Christian faith.

Although it was not a legal requirement to provide religious instruction for pupils before the 1944 Education Act, it was generally held that religion was an essential element in life and, therefore, pupils should be taught about it. The revised *Cambridgeshire Syllabus* of 1939 regarded the teaching of Christianity as the cure for the social ills of the days: 'The most menacing thing about our civilisation is its lack of direction ... ancient certainties by which our fathers lived and died seem irrelevant and almost meaningless to the children who have to live from crisis to crisis. Our problem ... springs out of the old truth that the only Gospel by which men can live must be a big and positive thing'.

The 1944 Education Act

The 1944 Education Act extended secondary education to all pupils. It made school worship and teaching about religion a legal requirement in British schools for the first time. The Act applied to all county and voluntary schools but not to independent schools. The teaching of the subject was to be called Religious Instruction (RI) but, together, RI and worship constituted a pupil's Religious Education (RE). The Act identified a special place for religion in schools in its endeavour to restructure and rebuild the educational system for a post-war age. The rise of Nazism and the Second World War had called into question the values of the society in which people lived. A study of beliefs and moral values was seen as essential for national reconstruction at a time when the western world had been ravaged by war. An editorial in the *Times Educational Supplement* in October 1943 commented that, 'There was never more need than today for a searching examination of values upon which our lives as individuals and our life as a people should be based'. And, while speaking at a conference in 1942, Basil Yeaxlee commented that, 'As the child grew up he began to ask for the meaning of all he had learned; religious teaching was the key which would help him carry forward to a community which was a family, which was democratic, in which all sought the good of others, because all were the children of one Father' (1).

The 1944 Education Act

This stated that:

- Religious Instruction (RI) was to be given regularly to all pupils;
- RI was to be given according to an 'agreed syllabus'. Exceptions were made for aided or special agreement schools.
- All local authorities (LEAs) were to write their own agreed syllabus or adopt one prepared by another local authority;
- The syllabuses were to be written by an 'Agreed Syllabus Conference' (ASC). This conference consisted of four panels, representing the Church of England, other religious denominations, the LEA and teachers' associations;
- The LEA could set up a Standing Advisory Council on Religious Education (SACRE) to help it carry out its duties;
- RI was made subject to formal inspection;
- Parents could ask for their children to be withdrawn from religious instruction on reasons of religious conscience. They could also ask, under certain conditions, that their children be given religious instruction different from that normally provided in the school (i.e. according to a particular faith tradition);
- Teachers could withdraw from agreeing to teach religious instruction.

The 1944 Act did not lay down what the content of religious instruction was to be. This was to be the responsibility of the Agreed Syllabus Conferences. However, it would appear correct to assume that it was believed that Christianity was the only faith which pupils would encounter. The consensus was that the values of education and the content of religious instruction in maintained schools would be Christian. Schools were simply assumed to be Christian communities that readily undertook the task of Christian education. Although it was not mentioned, it was assumed that the Cowper-Temple clause still applied. The Act had several weaknesses which, in the future, were to create problems for the teaching of the subject. Firstly, it omitted to say whether all pupils should receive religious instruction or only those who were below the statutory school-leaving age. Secondly, it failed to say how much curriculum time was to be given to RI and, thirdly, although religious instruction could now form part of a main subject in the teachers' certificate, there was no clarity as to what qualifications were necessary in order to be allowed to teach it.

There were a few dissenting voices. A leading article in the *Times Educational Supplement* argued that, 'if it is by no means certain yet that the basic philosophy of England will be in the future a Christian philosophy - which not unimportant sections of the community consciously and deliberately reject - any attempt to capture the schools for the systematic inculcation of the Christian view of life would be wrong and might well precipitate embittered conflict between rival religious and political parties for possession of the schools' (2).

Changes in Society 1944-1988

The emphasis on nurturing in the 1944 Education Act was significant. The 1949 edition of the *Cambridgeshire Syllabus* commented that, 'while the teacher should teach and not preach, in the classroom he should have an ever-present sense of responsibility so that, by his teaching, children may be led into the way of truth'. This reflected a contemporary practice that had been both formalised and reinforced by the Act. However, during the years between the two major Education Acts of this century, a number of changes in educational theory, theological and moral thinking, and in the make up of society brought about a series of developments in the nature of RI. Not all of these changes were universally welcomed and it remains questionable as to how far the Education Reform Act of 1988 took account of them.

Secularisation

By the 1950s, church-going was decreasing in the population and the process of secularisation was increasing. The requirements of the 1944 Act appeared to be having little success in encouraging people to return to the Christian tradition. Instead, by the end of the 1950s, the figures for juvenile delinquency were increasing and there was a general disrespect for traditional forms of authority. Although pupils commented that they were interested in some of the issues which religious instruction raised, they also said that the manner in which it was taught was largely irrelevant to their needs and circumstances (3). Religious instruction was undergoing a credibility crisis. Research by the educationalist Harold Loukes (4), in 1961, showed that pupils were not remembering much of what they were being taught and were misunderstanding some of the material. Edwin Cox (5) suggested that: 'The cause of this failure of communication probably lay in the nature of the provisions for religious education. The legislators may have been right in thinking that the basic religion of the country was still Christianity, and there was strong support in the population that children should be given the opportunity in schools of learning what Christianity was about, but what most understood by Christianity was not a highly theological, sacramental, Bible-based religion, but something more generalised, a kind of folk faith, a respect for the main Christian ethical tenets, which involved generosity, kindliness, tolerance and decent neighbourliness, but had little use for careful doctrinal definitions, for the minutiae of liturgical procedure, or for delving into the intricacies of Biblical scholarship'. Once educationalists recognised the growing secularisation of society and the ineffectiveness of much of religious instruction, they started to recommend changes in order to make the teaching more relevant to the pupils. These changes went hand in hand with other discoveries concerned with how children learn.

Pedagogical developments

In the 1960s, R J Goldman, K E Hyde and others researched into how children understand religious ideas. They concluded that religious thinking broadly followed the pattern of other thinking as described by Piaget, which implies that pupils are not ready for formal abstract thinking until their early teens. Until they reach this final stage of abstract thinking, they are not able to understand the complexities of symbolic and metaphysical language. So, if they are taught abstract concepts too early, there is a good chance that they will misunderstand them and carry this misunderstanding on into their adolescence and later. This can result in their religious ideas conflicting with the logico-scientific world view, creating conflict and, possibly, the rejection of the religious world view. This research raised the question of whether it was appropriate to teach abstract ideas in the early years of education. Also, it suggested that approaches which presented religion (i.e. Christianity) as a series of doctrines or biblical accounts to be learnt were not meeting the needs of pupils who would more profitably benefit from a child-centred and questioning approach. Goldman was not advocating that the aims of RI as Christian education should be changed but was challenging its methodology. These pedagogical developments coincided with theological questionings in the 1960s.

Theological developments

In 1963, Bishop John Robinson caused a theological storm when he published *Honest to God*. In his book, and for the first time, he introduced a wider audience to the theological questionings of Bultmann, Tillich and Bonhoeffer. *Honest to God* questioned traditional ways of speaking about God and encouraged individual personal quests in the search for truth. This development in theology had implications for religious instruction. Firstly, it cast doubts on some of the confessionally-based presentation of traditional theological formulations. Secondly, as Cox (6) has noted, it encouraged a person-centred approach to the search for meaning and truth in the sense that, 'this redefinition of religion suggested what the new content of religious education was to be, namely helping pupils to discover their deepest concern and to think out their personal and social problems in the light of it'. Around this time, the influential educationalist Harold Loukes started to write curriculum materials based on life themes that also made the subject more child-centred and in which religious instruction was regarded as a tool to help pupils discover significance and meaning in their own lives. This approach came to be known as the 'implicit religion approach'. It did not, however, last long - partly because pupils found that it lacked depth and sophistication, and partly because a new phenomena was growing in Britain to which RI would have to adapt itself. That phenomena was religious pluralism.

Pluralism

Immigrants from Commonwealth states had been arriving in Britain in considerable numbers since the 1950s but, in the late 1960s and early 1970s, their presence began to have a cultural impact as Britain started to move slowly towards becoming a pluralistic, multi-faith country. In addition, an increase in foreign travel and tourism meant that more people were coming into contact with different cultures and religions. There was a growing need to teach pupils about the different world religions that many were coming into contact with on a daily basis.

Phenomenological approaches

Most agreed syllabuses in the 1970s and 1980s turned away from confessional approaches and adopted a phenomenological approach. The leading exponent of this approach was Ninian Smart, who summed up the aim of RI as 'creating in pupils certain capacities to understand and think about religion'. Such an approach encouraged critical inquiry. Smart argued that an effective introduction to religious understanding had to contain references to the multi-dimensional nature of religion. In this way, religion could become a subject for objective study. This was a radical shift, supported by Smart's assertion that few schools could claim to be Christian communities since significant numbers of staff and pupils were not practising Christians. In an article, published in 1962, Smart wrote that 'neither Christians nor others can nowadays afford to go on living in a culturally isolated world' (7). At around the same time, the subject came to be known more widely as RE - as opposed to RI - since the latter title was associated with the confessional approaches now thought to be inappropriate in a pluralistic society.

In 1971, a Schools Council Working Paper (8), introduced Smart's ideas to an education audience. The first agreed syllabus to advocate the teaching of world religions was the *Birmingham Agreed Syllabus* of 1975. This was a controversial syllabus since it also included non-religious stances such as Marxism and Humanism. Soon, many other local authorities were to adopt a similar approach. Smart was instrumental in the planning of a conference at Shap Wells Hotel in 1969 on 'Comparative Religion in Education'. From this event sprang the annual, and at times bi-annual, SHAP conferences, together with numerous publications and curriculum materials. Not only was the content of RE changing but also the attitude, as it became accepted that it was not only appropriate to teach about the principal world religions but also that the enterprise was valid because all religions had elements of truth within them.

The phenomenological approach did not ask pupils to evaluate the truth claims of the religions. Instead, it proposed an external study of the dimensions of world faiths. These dimensions were what provided the conceptual framework for the study of religions and they emphasised their similarities. However, such freedom was accompanied by the danger that, without a study of truth claims, religion could be viewed as merely a matter of ritual and celebration so that the pupil became a tourist and the religions - which at their heart are life-changing institutions - were trivialised.

In the late 1970s and throughout the 1980s, the phenomenological approach came under attack. Members of the Religious Experience Research Unit (RERU) became concerned that, in many schools, it had led to a teaching of externals and had failed to allow pupils to come into contact with the spiritual dimension of religion. RERU's research showed that many people felt that they had experienced a spiritual dimension in life yet, in their view, RE was not taking enough notice of such experiences. Their books encouraged an exploration of such spiritual dimensions (9). Meanwhile, Michael Grimmitt (10) argued that the phenomenological approach could easily become 'multi-fact' religious 'education'. He suggested that RE should more directly promote the personal development of pupils.

Despite these criticisms of its approach, RE was a growth area in many parts of the country throughout the 1980s, especially in local authorities that had a subject adviser who could offer counsel and co-ordinate training opportunities for teachers. In 1985, the Swann Report, *Education for All*, congratulated RE on being the only subject to consistently introduce pupils to the racial diversity of British society. However, not everything was rosy. In the same year, the Secretary of State for Education, Keith Joseph, published a critical HMI Report on the position of RE in the last two years of compulsory schooling (11). It concluded that, 'the effectiveness of the contribution religious education can make to the curriculum is often limited by an insufficient allocation of time, resources and qualified staff'.

The 1988 Education Reform Act

The Education Reform Act 1988 (ERA) was intended to reinforce and clarify the 1944 Education Act with regard to collective worship and RE and to make its requirements more applicable to the changed situation in Britain. While it is fair to recognise that many of the proposals affirmed and reinforced current trends in RE teaching, controversy reigned over the politicising of some of the requirements.

The 1988 Education Act and DfE Circular: 1/94

This Act and Circular:

- Changed the term Religious Instruction to Religious Education;
- Described RE as part of the basic curriculum and reaffirmed that it was compulsory for all pupils aged 5-19 in maintained schools. Nursery schools and tertiary colleges were exempted and special schools required to do 'as far as is practicable';
- Made it clear that pupils should study other principal religious traditions in England in addition to Christianity;
- Required schools to follow an agreed syllabus. This clause included voluntary-controlled Church of England schools but provided flexible arrangements for voluntary-aided Church of England schools where provision for RE is determined by the governors. Catholic schools were to follow the Catholic Diocesan Syllabus;
- Allowed parents to withdraw their children from RE;
- Gave no ruling on how much time should be given to RE teaching but stated that it must be sufficient for the agreed syllabus to be covered;
- Required each local authority to set up a Standing Advisory Council for RE (SACRE) to 'advise the authority upon such matters connected with religious worship in county schools and the religious education to be given in accordance with an agreed syllabus';
- Retained a modified version of the Cowper-Temple clause. Although syllabuses could not teach according to denominational catechisms, they were allowed to include a study of such denominational teaching.

The critics were led by Baroness Cox and Baroness Blatch who claimed that multi-faith RE had led to the 'dilution of Christian teaching in a multi-faith mishmash' and that the inclusion of secular world views in RE had presented pupils with 'a position of extreme relativism in which all belief systems are included in a value-free hotchpotch' (12). Baroness Cox declared her intention 'to restore in our schools the centrality of Christianity as the major spiritual tradition of this land'. She moved amendment No. 28 which stated that 'religious education in all maintained schools shall be predominantly Christian'. An HMI staff inspector concluded at the time that 'the subject has been caught up in the unfinished debate on British national identity. The present ambivalence of Conservative politicians over whether or not Britain is part of Europe is mirrored in the religious education debates, where Christian is used as a code for White Anglo-Saxon and any teaching about the other religions of Britain is denounced emotionally as mishmash' (13). After concern about their interpretation, the requirements for collective worship were later clarified in DfE *Circular 1/94*.

Unlike other subjects in the new curriculum, RE was not subject to national attainment targets. Its content and approach was to be determined by the agreed syllabus, a diocesan syllabus or an independent schools' syllabus. Each local authority would have an agreed syllabus - either developed by its ASC or adopted from another authority. John Hull has argued that one of the main reasons why the government did not want RE to be part of the national curriculum was that it was thought to be undesirable for the Secretary of State for Education to have to adjudicate on matters concerning content and methods for the teaching of RE. Also, the 1988 Act stated that pupils could not be withdrawn from national curriculum classes but it was still important to retain the withdrawal clause for pupils who, on grounds of religion or conscience, did not want to subscribe to RE lessons. However, the fact that RE was not part of the formal curriculum led to much argument and, some would argue, a lack of status for RE. In June 1992, the Archbishop of York, the Right Reverend John Hapgood, raised the issue of RE being reintroduced into the national curriculum and this intervention led eventually to the writing of the SCAA Model Syllabuses for RE.

Following the inclusion of amendment 28 there has been much debate as to the meaning of the words, 'that the religious traditions in Great Britain are in the main Christian'. It raises the question of what percentages of time are to be spent on the teaching of Christianity and what on the other principal world faiths. Some commentators have suggested that the use of the words, '*whilst taking account of* the teaching and practices of the other principal religions' places other world religions in a subservient role to Christianity. In 1989, Edwin Cox commented that, 'reading the Act it is easy to get the impression that the government has not been much influenced by the changes that have occurred since 1944, but has been content to repeat and strengthen the religious clauses of the earlier Act, while making some allowance for the coming of religious pluralism' (14). However, it has also been suggested that the references to Christianity in the Act are aimed at redressing the imbalance between the teaching of Christianity and other world religions. It has been suggested that in the 1980s many teachers were finding resistance to their teaching of Christianity and, therefore, started to teach more and more world faith syllabuses due to the appeal of the new and exotic.

As a result of the wording of the ERA, formal complaints were made against the agreed syllabuses of Ealing and Newham. They were charged with being illegal since they did not devote sufficient time to the teaching of Christianity. Although this attempt to impose a Christian biased syllabus on two fiercely multi-racial boroughs failed, it did lead to the publication of a letter from the Department of Education and Science, in March 1991. ruling that agreed syllabuses should not be vague and 'must devote a reasonable amount of attention to teaching based on Christian traditions ... and the fact that the religious traditions in Great Britain are in the main Christian would in most cases be properly reflected by devoting most attention to Christian traditions' (15).

Although, the ERA led to controversy in a number of areas, it is important to note that benefits have accrued from its implementation as well. Firstly, RE was given a new importance. Once the legislation was imposed, all local authorities had to have their own agreed syllabus. Local authorities which had failed to produce an up-to-date syllabus started to do so. There began what Robson calls 'a brief golden age of new

Agreed Syllabus activity. Advisers were appointed where, in many cases, none had existed' (16). Secondly, the subject was forced into a position of questioning its assessment procedures. The national curriculum had included assessment procedures for all subjects and RE was not to be left behind. Two projects - the FARE Project (17) and the Westhill Project (18) - produced assessment guidelines for RE and led many agreed syllabuses to focus more closely on assessment procedures. And, finally, a national debate on RE was set in motion. The National Curriculum Council (NCC) started to take a greater interest and responsibility for RE. Under David Pascall, the agency began to work towards producing national guidelines for RE - a process that resulted in the publication in July 1994 of the SCAA Model Syllabuses for RE.

RE and the National Curriculum 1988-96

In 1992, the NCC, shortly to be merged with SEAC to form the Schools Curriculum and Assessment Authority (SCAA), commissioned the writing of national Model Syllabuses for RE. Working groups were formed which brought together members of the six major religious traditions in Britain, teachers, educationalists and government representatives. For the first time, representatives of the faith traditions were invited to select areas of their religion for pupils to study and to produce a report detailing what they thought each pupil should learn in any given key stage. Their *Faith Communities' Working Group Reports*, the two *Model Syllabuses* and a *Glossary* of terms were launched in July 1994.

Model syllabuses

The models suggested that the major world religions were to be taught at all key stages and that the content of these syllabuses was authorised by the faith communities themselves. The Model Syllabuses were not mandatory. Instead, the Standing Conferences directed to write or revise a local authority agreed syllabus, were encouraged to use them as a basis for advice on what should be included. The Model Syllabuses emphasised the discrete teaching of religions as opposed to thematic approaches. There was a critical reaction to this which led to the production of a third Model Syllabus by a group of lecturers in colleges of higher education. This model presented a structured thematic syllabus based around ultimate questions and has been used by some local authorities in revising or planning for their own syllabuses.

Subject status

On a parallel track, RE professionals lobbied the government to address the problem of the marginalisation of RE especially at key stage 4. SCAA was asked to consider a number of issues which led to the marginalisation of the subject at this level including staff shortages, lack of curriculum time, the lack of accreditation for compulsory core RE and the lack of status accorded the subject by some senior managers in schools. In response, SCAA and the new Department for Education and Employment (DfEE) offered accreditation for pupil learning in RE at key stage 4, and the five GCSE examining boards in England and Wales produced syllabuses for GCSE RE (short) courses. These new courses were designed to be taught across the full GCSE grade range from A* to G, in about 5% of curriculum time. The first examinations were scheduled for June 1997.

The RE adviser and OFSTED

The 'golden age' of the RE Adviser was short lived. The 1992 Education Act abolished the existing HMI structure and, in its place, established the Office for Standards in Education (OFSTED) with a new responsibility for statutory school inspection. Supported by a small number of HMI, OFSTED accredits inspectors who either work independently by being linked to one or more contracting agencies, or act as part of an LEA team. So, since 1992, many RE Advisers have become OFSTED-trained inspectors. On the same time-scale, budget delegation to schools has increased allowing them to develop professionally through selecting advice and consultancy from a range of sources. As a consequence, the opportunities for subsidised training - provided by local authorities and led by an RE Adviser - have been greatly reduced. However, the system of inspection has been good for RE in several ways. RE is treated in exactly the same way as other subjects and, if a school's provision for RE does not meet statutory requirements, then it becomes a key issue for action where the governors have to introduce an action plan for improvement. There is little doubt that some schools have improved their provision for RE as a result of an OFSTED inspection and others have appointed extra staff.

Current Issues

For schools, four questions dominate current discussions about religious education. The first is what can be done to improve professional standards? The ERA requires that all pupils at maintained schools should be taught RE including those in the sixth form. Many LEA agreed syllabuses are becoming more prescriptive and many schools are adopting the GCSE Short Course as a way of delivering the compulsory RE component in years 10 & 11. All of these developments place greater demands on the RE teacher but, in many schools, the subject is still being taught by non-specialists. Although the DfEE has recognised RE as a staff shortage subject for a number of years, the profession still requires more qualified teachers and better inservice training.

The second question asks what is the correct professional relationship between a teacher's personal faith and his or her role as an educator? There is a danger that RE could still be hijacked by those who wish to turn it into a secular neutral subject and this is particularly likely to happen when the case for Christianity has been politicised. The third question to pose is whether local authorities and schools have yet managed to find the right balance between Christianity and the other principal faith traditions because in some areas there is still discord and uncertainty. And, finally, with so much recent emphasis on the need for all subjects to contribute to the promotion of the spiritual, moral, social and cultural development of pupils, it is fair to ask what RE can, and should, contribute in this area.

NOTES:

1. Yeaxlee B, 1942, quoted in Religion in Education Vol. 9, No. 4 October 1942.
2. Hamilton H, 1942, *What is Religious Education?* Times Educational Supplement, 18 November 1942.
3. See, for example, a 1961 report by the Sheffield Institute of Education, *RE in Secondary Schools*, quoted in Loukes H, 1961, *Teenage Religion*.
4. Loukes H, 1961, *Teenage Religion*, London, SCM.
5. Cox E & Cairns J, 1989, *Reforming Religious Education*, Kogan Page.
6. Cox E, 1983, *Problems and Possibilities in Religious Education*.
7. Smart N, 1962, *The Christian and Other Religions*, Learning for Living Volume 1, Number 3.
8. Schools Council Working Paper, 1971, *Religious Education in Secondary Schools*.

9. See, for example, Robinson E, 1977, *The Original Vision*; Hay D, 1982, *Exploring Inner Space*; Hammond J, Hay J et al., 1990, *New Methods in R E Teaching: An Experiential Approach*.

10. Grimmitt M, 1987, *Religious Education and Personal Development*.

11. HMI, 1985, *A Survey of Religious Education in Years 4 and 5 of the Secondary School*.

12. House of Lords Official Report: Fifth Series, Volume 493, columns 1455 and 1456.

13. Robson G, 1996, quoting Hull and Jackson in *Religious Education, Government Policy and Professional Practice, 1985-1995*, British Journal of Religious Education Volume 19, Number 1.

14. Cox E and Cairns J, 1989, *Reforming Religious Education*, Kogan Page.

15. DES Letter to Chief Education Officers in England from Mr A Chamier, March 1991.

16. Robson G, 1996, *Religious Education, Government Policy and Professional Practice, 1985-1995*, British Journal of Religious Education Volume 19, Number 1, 1996.

17. Attainment in RE, Fare Project Report, 1989.

18. Assessing, Recording and Reporting RE, Westhill Project, 1991.

Section 2.
THE LEGAL
REQUIREMENTS

This section briefly summarises the current requirements for religious education in maintained and non-maintained schools.

The legal requirement for RE in county maintained schools is regulated by the 1988 and 1993 Education Acts. A subsequent DfE Circular (*DfE Circular 1/94*, HMSO, 1994) gave further advice and interpretation.

LEGAL REQUIREMENTS FOR MAINTAINED SCHOOLS		
	Legal requirements in the Education Reform Act (1988) and Education Act (1993)	**Additional advice on interpretation in DfE 1/94**
THE REQUIREMENT	The subject is referred to as 'religious education'. The curriculum for every maintained school shall comprise 'a basic curriculum which includes (a) provision for religious education for all registered pupils at the school' (1988, Section 2.1).	'RE, as part of the basic curriculum, should be provided for all registered pupils attending a maintained school' (paragraph 17) ... 'this includes those in reception classes and sixth forms, and is not confined to pupils of compulsory school age' (paragraph 20).
PUPIL & TEACHER RIGHTS OF WITHDRAWAL	Parents or guardians have the right to withdraw their children from religious education. 'If the parent of any pupil in attendance at any maintained school requests that he may be wholly or partly excused ... from receiving religious education given in the school ... the pupil shall be excused accordingly until the request is withdrawn' (1988, Section 9.1). In such an event the school has to be responsible for the supervision of any children withdrawn unless the children are lawfully receiving religious education elsewhere (1988, Section 44.2). Teachers may also withdraw from teaching religious education.	It is the headteacher's duty to secure this provision (paragraph 18). 'The headteacher and governing body must ensure that sufficient time and resources are given to RE in school to meet the statutory requirements' (paragraph 19). 'Conferences should ensure the syllabus has sufficient rigor and depth. They may find it helpful to note the assumptions made in Sir Ron Dearing's final report on the assessment on the time to be allotted to RE.. His recommendations assume ... 45 (hours) per year at key stage 3, and around 5 per cent of total curriculum time at key stage 4. The SCAA draft model syllabuses also assume around 40 hours per year' (paragraph 39).

	Legal requirements in the Education Reform Act (1988) and Education Act (1993)
ROLE OF THE SACRE and SYLLABUS REVIEW	Standing advisory councils on religious education: 'It shall be the duty of every local education authority to constitute a standing advisory council on religious education ... to advise the authority upon such matters connected with ... religious education to be given in accordance with the agreed syllabus as the authority may refer to the council or as the council may see fit' (1988, Section 11.1). 'Such matters include particular methods of teaching, the choice of materials and the provision of training for teachers' (1988, Section 11.2). 'The SACRE can also require a review of the agreed syllabus' (1988, Section 11.7). Membership of the SACRE represents '(a) such Christian and other religious denominations as, in the opinion of the authority, will appropriately reflect the principal religious traditions in the area; (b) except in the case of an area in Wales, the Church of England; (c) such associations representing teachers as, in the opinion of the authority, ought, having regard to the circumstances of the area, to be represented; and (d) the authority' (1988, Section 11.4). The 1993 Act alters the composition of both a SACRE and an agreed syllabus conference to include, under certain circumstances a fifth group or committee - the governing bodies of those grant-maintained schools equivalent to county or voluntary controlled schools (1993, paragraph 105). The 1993 Education Act requires every local education authority to institute a review of its locally agreed syllabus within five years of the last review, and subsequently every five years after the completion of each further review (1993, paragraph 29).

DEFINED AIMS, STATUS AND CONTENT

	Main legal requirements in the Education Reform Act (1988) and Education Act (1993)	**Additional advice on interpretation in DfE 1/94**
AIMS	As part of the total curriculum, religious education should also promote the 'spiritual, moral, cultural, mental and physical development of pupils and of society' (Section 1.2).	The following aims are referred to: 'Religious education in schools should seek: to develop pupils' knowledge, understanding and awareness of Christianity, as the predominant religion in Great Britain, and the other principal religions represented in the country' and .... 'to help promote pupils' spiritual, moral, cultural and mental development' (paragraph 16).

THE STATUS OF RE	RE is part of the basic curriculum (Section 2.1a).	'The special status of RE as part of the basic but not the national curriculum is important. It ensures that RE has equal standing in relation to national curriculum subjects within a school's curriculum, but is not subject to statutorily prescribed national attainment targets, programmes of study and assessment arrangements' (paragraph 20). However, 'an agreed syllabus conference may recommend the inclusion of attainment targets, programmes of study and assessment arrangements in locally determined form in its proposals' (paragraph 37).
THE CONTENT OF RE	For county maintained schools, RE must be in accordance with the locally agreed syllabus of the local education authority in whose area they are situated. 'A syllabus must give sufficient particulars of what is to be taught for it to be clear that the teaching carried out in pursuance of that syllabus would be consistent with the requirement (that it must reflect the fact that the religious traditions in Great Britain are in the main Christian whilst taking account of the teaching and practices of the other principal religions represented in Great Britain' (Section 8.3). Agreed syllabuses must be non-denominational. However, teaching about a particular catechism or formulary is not prohibited. 'No ... syllabus shall provide for religious education to be given to pupils at such a school by means of any catechism or formulary which is distinctive of any particular religious denomination; but this provision is not to be taken as prohibiting in such a syllabus for the study of such catechisms or formularies' (1988, Schedule 1).	'Syllabuses must not be designed to convert pupils, or urge a particular religion or religious belief on pupils' (paragraph 32). It is not enough simply to be able to say that the teaching might be capable of meeting those requirements' (paragraph 33). 'The syllabus should indicate at what ages or stages the particular subject matter in relation to each religion should be taught' (paragraph 34). 'As a whole and at each key stage, the relative content devoted to Christianity in the syllabus should predominate' (paragraph 35). 'The syllabus should not be confined to information about religions and religious traditions, practices and teaching, but extend in a religious context to wider areas of morality, including the way in which people's religious beliefs and practices affect their understanding of moral issues and the consequences their behaviour has upon the family and society' (paragraph 36).

Many independent schools have a church foundation. Sometimes independent schools will be required to follow the diocesan agreed syllabus. At other times, guidelines for the syllabus will be laid down in the trust deeds of the school. While independent schools have the freedom to select their own syllabus, in May 1994, the Independent Schools' RE Syllabus was launched (see the *Resource Guide* for more details).

LEGAL REQUIREMENTS FOR OTHER SCHOOLS

Special schools: 'Arrangements shall be made to secure that, so far as practicable, every pupil attending the school will ... receive religious education, or will be withdrawn from ... receiving such education, in accordance with the wishes of his parent' (*Education Special Schools Regulations 1994*, Section II. 10).

Sixth form colleges: Colleges who were under school regulation until 30th September 1992 are required to provide religious education for all students who wish to receive it (*Further and Higher Education Act 1992*, Section 45). A college governing body will be considered to be fulfilling their responsibilities if religious education is provided when it is convenient for the majority of full-time students to attend (Section 45.3). The governing body of a sixth form college decides the content of religious education.

Grant-maintained schools: Parents of pupils at a grant-maintained school which was a controlled school immediately before it became a grant-maintained school, can request religious education for their children, but 'not more than two periods in each week' (*Education Reform Act 1988*, Section 85.2). A grant-maintained school may follow the locally agreed syllabus of any local education authority in England and Wales, so long as that syllabus meets the 1988 Act's requirements (*Education Act 1993*, Section W.142).

Voluntary-controlled schools: The RE offered is to be in accordance with the LEA's locally agreed syllabus. However parents can request that the RE provided for their children be in accordance with any trust deed or the practice followed before the school became controlled (*Education Act 1944*, Section 27).

Voluntary-aided and special agreement schools: The RE is 'to be determined by the governors in accordance with the trust deed in line with practice before the school became a voluntary school. But, provision in accordance with the LEA's locally agreed syllabus may be made where parents request it' (*Education Act 1944*, Section 28).

City Technology Colleges: 'The provisions of the Education Acts relating to religious education ... do not apply to city technology colleges and city colleges for the technology of the arts. These schools are independent schools but, as a condition of grant, they are required to make provision for religious education ... which is broadly in line with that in maintained schools. The requirements are set down in the funding agreements' (*DfE Circular 1/94*, Annex C).

Church-aided schools: Take advice from their diocese. Many dioceses have their own RE syllabus.

Section 3.
AIMS AND APPROACHES

Religious Education has often been regarded as having a questionable status within the school curriculum. The subject has sometimes been likened to a parasite, draining important teaching time from what are supposed to be more important, academic and useful subjects. In order to counteract such negative images, this section helps teachers of RE to develop clear and well-publicised aims for their subject.

Aims for RE

When writing a departmental RE policy document or reviewing aims and objectives, it is necessary to take into consideration the Locally Agreed Syllabus, Diocesan Syllabus or the Independent Schools Syllabus which the school is following. The chart below shows some of the disparate aims proposed for RE. It is important to reach a consensus within a department and to decide which of these aims are unique to RE and which, if adopted, might be counter-productive. It is worth asking whether any of these aims actually run contrary to the department's view of what RE should be doing, whether their delivery could be unprofessional, and whether their adoption will ensure that RE helps to develop pupils in a unique way. For example, one issue to consider is the relationship between learning about religion and learning from religion and how pupils are to learn from a religion without being indoctrinated into it.

Aims For RE

Aims for RE may include the following:

- to educate pupils for the world in which they live;
- to help pupils understand the multicultural and multi-faith society in which they live;
- to encourage pupils to understand a religion from the point of view of an adherent;
- to help pupils reflect upon their own needs, experiences and questions and to confront what are sometimes referred to as 'ultimate questions';
- to expand pupils' ways of looking at the world;
- to teach morality;
- to give pupils the skills to make meaningful judgements between conflicting beliefs and values;
- to enable pupils to understand the nature of religious beliefs and practices;
- to teach tolerance towards people of different faiths;
- to enable pupils to understand the importance and influence of religious beliefs and practices in the lives of believers;
- to encourage pupils to make their own assessment of religion;
- to encourage pupils to search for truth;
- to help pupils to understand the foundations upon which some of the world's great civilisations have been built;

- to reflect on and respond to the spiritual dimension of life;
- to help pupils in a personal search for meaning;
- to educate pupils in an academic discipline;
- to teach pupils how to use religious language (including symbol, image and analogy);
- to enable pupils to think religiously and become religiously literate;
- to explore world views, including non-religious stances in life such as secularism and humanism;
- to help pupils recognise their own 'tacit religion';
- to help pupils discuss personal and social issues such as the role of the family and responsibility for the world;
- to educate pupils in the religious heritage of their country;
- to teach pupils the difference between right and wrong and to apply this to life.

Approaches to Teaching RE

During the last thirty years, there have been numerous approaches to the teaching of world religions. These have resulted in the publication of a wide range of curriculum materials. Some approaches have been developed into complete series of books for different key stages. However, new approaches are being researched all the time. All those discussed below have insights to offer and no single approach is right or wrong. The best advice for a department is to capitalise on the best aspects of each one. Aware of this, some schools buy individual sets of a number of different books, or even half sets and use them to complement each other.

The Phenomenological Approach

The leading exponent of this approach was Ninian Smart. He encouraged critical inquiry into religion arguing that 'an effective introduction to religious understanding had to contain references to the multi-dimensional nature of religion'. These dimensions were called the phenomenon of religion. The aim of this objective study of religion was to understand a religion from the point of view of the adherent of the faith, to 'step inside their shoes' and to understand the religion from their point of view. This approach has also been called 'the explicit religion approach'. It was extremely influential in the 1970s and 1980s both in the writing of agreed syllabuses and in the production of curriculum materials. A leading institution in this area is Westhill College, Birmingham, which has produced curriculum books, photographic packs and held inservice training courses in which teachers and pupils have been encouraged to visit adherents of faith communities in their own communities and places of worship.

The Experiential Approach

The experiential approach arose out of the work of the Religious Experience Research Project (now re-named the Religious Experience and Education Project). By the early 1980s, this project had collected enough research information to make it clear that very large numbers of people in Britain interpret some of their life experience in religious terms. The experiential approach aims to help pupils understand something of the ways in which people with spiritual experience understand the world, and that their own way of looking at the world is only one among many.

The approach is correctly located as an offshoot of the phenomenological. It developed out of an anxiety that the phenomenological approach had come to be taught in many schools as a concentration on external, public phenomena. Hammond and Hay (1) argued that, 'to concentrate on externals such as discussions of doctrine, moral stances, pilgrimages, rituals and so on, is to ignore the most central issue in religion - its spirituality'. For them, the experiential approach understands phenomenology as a direct investigation of peoples' experiences of religion and, for this to happen, it is important to take the phenomena of religion seriously because 'without an appreciation of the intentions of religious people, the publicly visible phenomena of their faith are likely to seem remote or meaningless to the pupil'. Therefore, in order to understand the inner world of a religious believer, this approach teaches the need for each pupil to appreciate their own inner world of experience. One consequence is to pay more attention to the spiritual dimension of religion and the available curriculum material offers a methodology for doing this in an educationally responsible way.

The Conceptual Approach

A report from Westhill College in 1991 (2) claimed that, 'concepts are the main focal point of any educational programme' and 'help us to make sense of what we observe and encounter in particular religions'. The approach drew on the work of Jerome Bruner, a post-Piagetian, who advocated a conceptual approach to the teaching of all subjects so that, 'the curriculum of a subject should be determined by the most fundamental understanding that can be achieved of the underlying principles that give structure to that subject'. Bruner went on to argue that concepts can be taught at any age as long as they are communicated in a manner appropriate to the thought patterns of the child. Kincaid (3) suggested that concepts become the 'advance organisers' around which other religious material can be grouped and the 'pegs' on which other material hangs. So, this approach attempts to engage pupils with the world view of a particular religion. It is based upon a belief that each world religion offers a distinctive world view which can be understood through its key beliefs. Approaching a religion by means of key beliefs enables pupils to enter into the world view of the believer.

The Stapleford Project has pioneered this way of looking at RE. Its planning process has been compared to putting together a jigsaw. Before assembling a jigsaw, it helps to organise individual pieces around its main areas so, for example, all the blue pieces are put together to form the sky. So, too, with a religion. A religious world view is made up of its distinctive beliefs. Each belief is itself made up of a number of pieces or concepts and it is necessary to 'crack open' the belief into its 'concept cluster'. Each of these concepts can then form the focus of a different approach to the belief with different year groups. Once the belief has been unpacked and a particular concept chosen for exploration, the next stage is to find a purchase point between the belief and the pupils' world views. The belief or concept is then explored from within the pupils' own frame of reference and the relevance of the concept for him or her is explored. This approach has also been described as 'content-structured and child-related'. Whilst it recognises the importance of learning about the beliefs of a religion, it encourages pupils to learn from the religion, by exploring and developing their own belief system. This is still an influential approach. The SCAA Model RE Syllabus 2, published in 1994, reflects it in the way in which each religion is organised around its key teachings.

The Thematic Approach

This approach teaches religious material by themes such as pilgrimage, religious buildings, sacred books or celebrations. Advocates of this approach recognise that care needs to be taken in order not to blur the distinctions between religions. However, it recognises that all world religions provide answers to some of the most searching questions facing humanity: issues about suffering, the nature of proof, the purpose of life and the end of life. It emphasises that all religions are concerned with this quest for meaning.

Within the thematic approach, some curriculum materials concentrate on explicit religious themes such as sacred books while others explore the life-themes approach which 'helps pupils explore an aspect of shared human experience in order to develop an understanding of that experience and the 'fundamental' or 'ultimate' questions it raises' (4). Such questions are explored from the point of view of a number of religions.

The Ethnographic Approach

The Warwick RE Project is one of a number of integrated projects undertaken by the Warwick Religions and Education Research Unit. This unit has three interests: an ethnographic study of religion in the community, theoretical work in religious education and the production of curriculum material for use in the classroom. These materials draw upon ethnographic studies of children's experience of religion. Whilst the project recognises the value of the SCAA *Faith Communities' Working Group Reports*, it questions the way in which each religion is categorised. The unit's Director, Robert Jackson, has argued (5) that the practice of 'carving up' religious life into a handful of 'world religions' which conform to a common system of beliefs and practices, ends with 'homogenised lists of agreed content' that 'cannot be viewed as effective or authentic representations of the religious traditions though they may prove to be a valuable aid to the deliberations of Agreed Syllabus Conferences'.

So, in contrast, the Warwick RE Project is an attempt to take serious note of the multiplicity of interpretations and expressions within a faith tradition. Its curriculum materials are built around ethnographic studies of children, interviews with them and their families, and consultation with local religious leaders and recognised consultants from within the religions. Judith Everington, Joint General Editor of the curriculum material *Bridges to Religions* and *Interpreting Religions* series, comments that 'the project team rejects the notion that a tradition can be reduced to an essence or set of fundamentals ... an authentic representation of a tradition is one which is effective in portraying the richness of its internal complexity and diversity'. The curriculum materials are, therefore, heavily based upon data obtained in the field of ethnographic research. The project has tried to avoid imposing upon this data any terminology or structure that stems from outside the traditions.

NOTES:

1. Hammond, Hay et al, 1990, *New Methods in RE Teaching: An experiential approach*, Oliver and Boyd.
2. *Assessing Recording and Reporting RE*, 1991, Regional RE Centre, Westhill College.
3. Kincaid, 1991, *Learning in RE*, Hodder and Stoughton.
4. Hasted S & Teece G, *Living Questions: Teacher's Resource Book*, Stanley Thornes.
5. Everington J, 1996, *A Question of Authenticity: The Relationship between Educators and Practitioners in the Representation of Religious Traditions*, British Journal of Religious Education Volume 18, Number 2.

Section 4.
EFFECTIVE TEACHING

This section moves from theory to practice and starts to address the teacher of RE directly. It raises five key issues that have to be resolved in the development of departmental policy and classroom pedagogy.

Issue 1: Pluralism

You find yourself working in a richly multicultural area. You teach pupils from all of the six principal world faiths as well as pupils from other faiths and life stances. What do you choose to teach in RE? How do you go about teaching it?

Whether or not you teach in a richly multicultural area, RE syllabuses today require a study of a number of different faiths. This poses a real challenge for the RE teacher who has to face a number of questions including, 'Which religions do you choose?', 'How much time do you spend on each religion?' and 'What kind of approach do you take towards the teaching of world faiths?'.

In practice, what is taught will be determined by a number of factors, including the requirements of your syllabus, your expertise and the resources which are available. However, there are a number of roles which you, as the RE teacher, can take in relation to the plurality of belief systems. Each role has a number of advantages and disadvantages. Some possible roles are set out below. Although they are presented here as distinct models, they are not always exclusive. In practice, teachers may consider it more appropriate to act as a neutral chair person for part of the time, such as when chairing a debate on a moral issue, but, at other times, be willing to speak about their own faith position such as when they are asked explicitly by pupils what they believe.

The Neutral Approach

Some teachers attempt to adopt a neutral approach in the presentation of world faiths. This approach allows pupils to 'tour' around the world faiths and study them all. It has some significant advantages in that it protects the pupil's autonomy and is non-confessional. However, critics suggest that the approach underemphasises the controversial nature of religious belief and truth claims because it presents religious commitment as a matter of personal choice. This contradicts the belief that faith is not a matter of personal choice but of revelation. They also argue that most pupils do not possess the skills to make rational choices or to draw distinctions between religions presented in this way.

The Explicit Approach

Other teachers believe it is impossible to be neutral and are explicit about their own faith position. This approach has the advantage that the teacher can show with enthusiasm how religious belief affects a person's whole life. However, critics of this approach point to a number of inherent dangers. Firstly, it is confessional and may be unethical in as much as the teacher fails to communicate to pupils the controversial nature of his or her beliefs - presenting them instead as the only valid ones. Secondly, it can ignore the important area of the controversial nature of religious truth claims and, thirdly, it is impractical in many classrooms where teenagers - used to being critical - are sensitive to any unquestioning presentation of beliefs.

The Committed Approach Many teachers, whether or not they are committed to a particular faith, nevertheless believe it is important for pupils to learn about the rich diversity of religious faith in the world today and attempt to present other faiths with respect and accuracy. Such an approach respects the integrity of the pupil to make his or her own choice, presents him or her with the plurality of evidence and recognises the controversial nature of religious belief. It also allows the teacher to express his or her own commitment whilst protecting pupil autonomy. Critics point out that it requires a lot of work by the teacher to teach each world faith accurately, the evidence selected can be biased and they question whether pupils can cope with a plurality of evidence.

Ways of teaching about world faiths

These are some ways that can help to introduce the study of world faiths that are not the teacher's own:

- Exploring new resources including books written by members of the faith tradition;
- Attendance at extra-mural and inservice courses on world faiths;
- Inviting visitors from different faith traditions to the school;
- Visiting faith communities;
- Using artefact boxes and resources.

Issue 2: Neutrality versus Commitment *You are a Christian RE teacher who believes that there is only one form of salvation, and that is through Jesus Christ. You feel that you need to communicate this to pupils without pressurising them into believing the same. How do you teach other religions which you don't believe in? How do you accept pupils' comments about your faith?*

Many RE teachers have their own personal beliefs which they hold dear. However, the key issue is the relationship between a teacher's personal faith commitment and the need for openness in their teaching. A particular point of difficulty arises over the treatment of truth claims, especially for those traditions which are most exclusivist in their approach.

Is there such a thing as neutrality? If so, is it desirable?

All teachers are in some sense the victims of their own commitments. The commitment of the teacher can affect his or her teaching even in the choice of syllabus. For example, the agnostic teacher's pursuit of objectivity and neutrality may reflect a studied commitment to a phenomenological evaluation of religion and not just a method of teaching. This is a commitment of a secular kind. Also, purely descriptive accounts of religion can be offensive. For example, a Muslim might view religious education as defective if pupils are obliged to learn about Islam instead of being helped to measure up to the difference that Islam could make in their lives. This suggests that a neutral approach to religion has a place in education but, perhaps, in developing historical awareness or developing cultural and social understanding rather than in RE itself.

Is religious commitment a desirable thing?

Commitment can be a valuable primary resource in the classroom. Firstly, it can give pupils a glimpse of the passion which is at the heart of many religious beliefs and illustrate for them the importance of religious belief in a person's life. Also, commitment is not merely one of the aspects of religion, it is ultimately what religion is about, and so the task of the RE teacher requires more than teaching about a religion - it has to deal with the experience of it as well. Secondly, it can be argued that teachers need to consciously recognise their own commitments and be willing to carry out a systematic investigation - so far as it is possible with pupils themselves - of the controversial nature of holding religious beliefs. And finally, in the absence of personal involvement on the part of the teacher and the taught, religions may appear as dull and irrelevant habits, rather than as lively options. But, on the other hand, religious commitment in the teacher can become dangerous if pupils are not allowed to question and search for themselves. If this happens the subject ceases to be educational and becomes instructional or even indoctrinating in its outlook. This is both unprofessional and unethical.

So, what is required of teachers?

First and foremost, teachers need to have an awareness of their own commitments, attitudes and prejudices and an awareness of the commitments, attitudes and prejudices of others. This probably comes from an acceptance of the fact that genuine neutrality is impossible. Secondly, teachers need to recognise that religion is a dynamic activity - a searching for truth which should be open to the questioning of their pupils. This argues that all RE teachers need to have a commitment to the search for truth rather than to any one set of beliefs, underlined by the fact that the concept of religious pluralism assumes a pluralism of commitments. However, as well as being willing to relate to others with different commitments, and respecting and valuing their insights, teachers may decide to declare their own personal commitments. This means that pupils are not left thinking that their teachers are somehow trying to be neutral and is a safeguard against charges of indoctrination.

What is the best way to do this?

The best approach is to present the evidence in favour of religious commitment in as challenging a way as possible through allowing pupils to engage critically with your commitment. It is also important to take care over language. A distinction needs to be made between matters of belief and matters of fact. Statements of belief need to be 'owned' or 'grounded'. To own a particular belief means to declare that 'I believe …' or 'It seems to me …' or 'In my experience …' the belief has truth or meaning. To ground a belief is to attach it to a group of people who hold it; for example, 'Christians believe that …' or 'It says in the Bible that …' or 'Orthodox Jews believe that …'. By owning, or grounding, a belief you are not assuming that it is true or authoritative for other people.

Issue 3: The Role of RE in the Broader Curriculum

'We train our children to become good technicians but we don't educate them to become good human beings'.

Dr. Michael Hartoonian

The 1988 Education Reform Act states that each subject of the curriculum has a responsibility for promoting the spiritual, moral, cultural, mental and physical development of pupils. The Act requires the curriculum to provide a 'balanced and broadly based curriculum which promotes the spiritual, moral, cultural, mental and physical development of pupils at the school and of society...' (*ERA 1988, Chapter 40.1*). The monitoring of this legal requirement is by OFSTED and is undertaken by inspectors using the agency's Inspection Schedule (*Guidance on the Inspection of Secondary Schools, London HMSO, OFSTED, 1995*). An RE department must possess a clear understanding of its part in meeting these requirements.

Spiritual Aspects

OFSTED asks: *Does the school provide its pupils with knowledge and insight into values and religious beliefs and enable them to reflect on their experiences in a way which develops their self-knowledge and spiritual awareness?*

Effective provision for spiritual development depends on a curriculum and approaches to teaching which embody clear values and provide opportunities for pupils to gain understanding by developing a sense of curiosity through reflection on their own and other people's lives and beliefs, their environment and the human condition. It relies on teachers receiving and valuing pupils' ideas across the whole curriculum, for example, in literature, art, music, history and RE. Acts of collective worship play a particular part. To the extent that spiritual insights imply an awareness of how pupils relate to others, there is a strong link to both moral and social development.

Although RE and spiritual development are not synonymous, the former can make a significant contribution to the latter. Inspectors might consider, for example, whether pupils are encouraged to consider life's fundamental questions and how religious teaching can relate to them; respond to such questions with reference to the teachings and practices of religions as well as from their own experience and viewpoint; and reflect on their own beliefs or values in the light of what they are studying in RE.

Moral Aspects

OFSTED asks: *Does the school teach the principles which separate right from wrong?*

The essence of moral development is to build a framework of values which regulate personal behaviour through principles, rather than through fear of punishment or regard. Pupils are able to make moral decisions through the application of reason, even though they may not cope quite so securely with problems in which they are emotionally involved. In other words, their learning about moral issues may be on a different plane from their behaviour. Moral and social education are loosely related and depend on the school fostering values such as honesty, fairness and respect for truth and justice.

Inspectors have to consider whether the school provides a moral code as a basis for behaviour which is promoted through the life of the school. They also look at the opportunities for pupils to develop and express moral values and extend social and personal understanding across a range of issues, including, for example, personal rights and responsibilities and equal opportunities. In all areas of the curriculum, pupils can be encouraged to explore their ideas about such issues. The moral and social issues raised through the study of warfare, the interaction of people, resources and the environment, and the ways in which science and technology can affect our lives, are typical examples. Sensitive discussion of incidents that arise in school, or outside, may be used to help pupils distinguish right from wrong behaviour.

Social Aspects

OFSTED asks: *Does the school encourage pupils to relate effectively to others, take responsibility, participate fully in the community and develop an understanding of citizenship?*

Social development hinges on an acceptance of group rules and the ability to set oneself in a wider context. Adolescents may find that their need to be socially compliant is sometimes at odds with their developing moral sensibility. Partly for this reason, the quality of relationships in schools is of crucial importance in forming pupils' attitudes to good social behaviour and self-discipline.

Inspectors have to consider how the school, through its organisation, curriculum and other activities, contributes to social development through experience and understanding of social relationships and the rights and responsibilities of individuals within the social setting. Evidence may include opportunities for pupils to work co-operatively in lessons, on projects or in games involving competition, discipline and fair play. Account should be taken of opportunities for pupils to take on responsibility, demonstrate initiative and contribute to the life of the school as a community. Vocational courses at key stage 4 and post-16 can play a significant part in this development.

Cultural Aspects

OFSTED asks: *Does the school teach pupils to appreciate and develop their own cultural traditions and appreciate the diversity and richness of other cultures?*

Cultural development is concerned with both participation in and appreciation of cultural traditions. The school's approach should be active. Inspectors look for evidence of how the school seeks to enrich its pupils' knowledge and experience of their own and other cultural traditions, through the curriculum and through visits, clubs and other activities. Aspects of the curriculum such as history, geography, art, music, dance, drama, literature and the study of language can all contribute positively, for example, through opportunities for pupils to visit museums and art galleries, work with artists, authors and performers, develop openness towards and value the music and dance of different cultures and appreciate the natural world through art and literature.

Following the Post-16 Review undertaken by Sir Ron Dearing in 1996, spiritual and moral issues are now being written into all A Level syllabuses. Moral issues are also written into national vocational qualifications. SCAA has established a Values Forum which has proposed that the authority should produce detailed guidance for schools on spiritual, moral, social and cultural development.

Issue 4: Teaching Moral Issues in RE

Many teachers choose to study moral issues with their pupils in RE lessons. Some schools undertake GCSE and A Level modules or examination papers which focus on religious perspectives on moral and ethical issues. Because of the prominent position which consideration of moral issues now takes in RE, teachers of the subject need a well-defined understanding of their aims and role. Two tragic incidents partly explain why the debate about the teaching of morals in schools has been placed so high on the educational and political agenda. These were the murders at a primary school in Dunblane in March 1996 and the murder of London headteacher Philip Lawrence in December 1995. Partly because of them, notice was taken of an OFSTED discussion paper (*Spiritual, Moral, Social and Cultural Development*, OFSTED, 1994) and SCAA, under the leadership of Dr Nicholas Tate, became further involved in 1996. One outcome was the formation of the National Forum on Values in Education and the Community after the success of a SCAA conference on 'Education for Adult Life'.

The aims of the Forum were to determine whether there was sufficient agreement in the community to draw up a common moral code through which schools might transmit moral values to pupils. It had 150 members drawn from a range of beliefs and different sectors of society. Their work resulted in the publication of a set of draft moral values. Under the headings of Society, Relationships, Self, and Environment, a set of 'principles for action' was summarised. In 1997, SCAA intends to finalise the principles and then to develop draft model syllabuses for moral, personal and social education (MPSE) along the same lines as those for religious education.

Whilst it has long been recognised that moral development is the responsibility of the whole school, it remains the case that RE has a privileged responsibility in focusing on the moral maze and needs to play its part in promoting the moral development of all pupils. Morality is about informed choices between right and wrong and, for pupils to be morally literate, they need to become aware of the moral dimensions of different situations, know moral values and what they require of people in concrete cases, and be able to make thoughtful moral decisions for themselves. However, morality cannot exist in a vacuum. It is based on a value system and each principal religion provides such a value system, a world view.

In July 1994, SCAA published, with the model RE syllabuses, the *Faith Communities' Working Group Reports*. These indicated the main elements of each religion's 'world view'. The model syllabuses went on to state the need for pupils to learn both from, and about, the religions they study. RE provides pupils with the opportunity of learning the world views of the principal religions and to consider religious responses to moral issues. It follows, therefore, that pupils should be encouraged to reflect on what they can learn from the different religious perspectives and to consider their own beliefs and values. However that assertion raises a number of issues for teachers. They include the following:

What message are you giving when you teach moral issues?

If you present a moral issue and the teachings from different world religions what are you saying to the pupil? Are you saying that all the different teachings of world religions are equally valid?

Is tolerance a virtue to be aimed at?

The question of tolerance and where it turns into moral relativism is a difficult one. In a review from the *Journal of Moral Education* (Kathleen Gow's 'Yes, Virginia, there is Right and Wrong', 1980), Don Locke sums it up: 'The trouble with the 'new' moral education ... is that it is actually amoral education. Under the guise of impartiality, non-directiveness, non-indoctrination and non-interference in the child's autonomy, Moral Values Education is in fact inculcating its own value perspective. What looks like a liberal tolerance of conflicting opinions is, in practice, education in moral relativism and individual utilitarianism'.

Are you providing the necessary tools for pupils to understand a religious perspective on morality?

Holy books are not law books and, therefore, should not be treated as such. Instead, they present a religious world view. Believers enter into this world view and think with, for example, a Buddhist or Christian mind. Pupils need to be given the opportunity of trying on the spectacles of these religions and seeing the world from a similar perspective. This can be done as effectively through story, poetry, parable and reflection as through learning the laws. There is a critical edge to this. For example, someone who was starting to think in a Christian way would subject opinions, statements and facts to scrutiny. They would be acquiring the skills to hypothesise and applying the key teachings and values of Jesus and the Church to the world in which they lived. Following this model, it is apparent that the issue for RE is not a matter of whether to learn a long list of facts or a set of biblical quotes. Instead pupils need to hold their own conversations with the material and to come to their own conclusions through critical reflective thinking.

How do you show the relevance of religious teachings to morality?

One way of doing this is by using case studies and biographies, to show how believers apply religious teaching on moral issues to their lives. Such case studies will also, hopefully, show how believers struggle to live out their religion. It is wrong to give pupils the impression that believers find moral issues easy.

How does the teaching of morality connect with the lives of pupils?

It is important to make links between a religious perspective on moral issues and the life of the pupils as a point of purchase into the pupils' worlds. Some moral questions will arise directly out of the pupils' own experiences. Is it ever right to lie? Is it always right to be loyal to your friends? However, other questions are less likely to. Is it ever right to go to war? Is euthanasia justified? Therefore, one way of introducing such issues is to contextualise them, perhaps by bringing in a relevant newspaper article or raising a moral issue which has been the focus of a television programme. Grouping moral questions around key topics helps pupils to focus on them and avoids applying religious teaching in an *ad hoc* manner. By grouping moral issues together, it is possible to explore the religious perspective on whole issues such as people's responsibility towards each other, responsibility for the environment and matters of life and death.

Is there a distinction between moral education and moral knowledge?

Ethics is made up of a number of strands: principles, skills, attitudes and dispositions. It has its own vocabulary and learning about a religion means being able to use the concepts associated with its beliefs and the discourse in which they are embedded. For example, Christian ethics involves a conceptual understanding of words like 'grace', 'judgement', 'mercy' and 'virtue' which goes beyond their everyday use. One way to explore this distinction is to encourage pupils to think through moral situations and to consider conflicting points of view. As a simple example, pupils can be asked to consider the moral acceptability of the different characters in the following story:

> *A girl is on her way to marry her fiancé. In order to do so, she must cross an unswimmable river and a labyrinthine forest for which she must have a guide. To cross the river she asks the boatman to take her. He replies that he will do so if she will make love to him. Distressed at this, and unable to decide what to do, she goes to a wise man for advice. The wise man simply tells her, 'I cannot help you'. Upon further reflection, she agrees to the boatman's offer and he takes her across. She then comes to the forest. The guide is the devil. He agrees to take her through on the same terms as stipulated by the boatman. Having agreed to the boatman she sees no point in sacrificing her aim now and does as the devil decrees. After passing through the forest she meets her fiancé and feels she must tell him of what has happened. On hearing about what she has done he refuses to marry her.*

Clive Erricker, who quoted this story in the *British Journal of Religious Education*, makes the following observation on the exercise: 'As an exercise, the characters in the story can be ranked in order of moral acceptability. With pupils, the order can vary substantially, though they are often initially unclear as to why. For example, many rank the girl top because it was she who made the greatest effort and sacrificed herself because of her love for her fiancé. Others rank the fiancé top because he stood by his moral principle that sex outside marriage is wrong. The wise man is sometimes ranked top because his was the moral virtue of blamelessness and he told the truth. The boatman tends to appeal to those with a sense of moral anarchy who believe that we are all fundamentally self-seeking and the boatman is not afraid to let this be known. The structure of the moral decision-making, and how a group have arrived at their judgements, can be explored from these initial statements'.

Issue 5: Differentiation in the RE Classroom

Differentiation refers to the ways in which teachers try to provide for the variations in the abilities, aptitudes, needs and interests of pupils. It is not about fragmenting a class into many groups all working on different subject matter. Rather it is individuals or groups working on different aspects, activities or levels of a particular theme or topic.

It is sometimes thought that differentiation is only necessary in mixed-ability classes. However, it is important to remember that even if pupils are placed in ability sets or banded there is still likely to be some range of ability within the group. Not only that, but pupils bring with them a range of experiences, interests, expectations, attitudes and needs. This presents a challenge for any teacher but particularly the RE teacher who will probably see each class only once a week. To be realistic, it will be at least half term, if not later, before the RE teacher can really get to know his or her pupils academically. Of course, this is made much easier if the same member of staff teaches the same class for two consecutive years. It is helpful to consider differentiation from four perspectives: planning lessons, classroom organisation, teachers and pupils. Under each of these headings, there are a number of questions to be answered in order to achieve differentiation within the RE classroom. These are summarised in the charts on the following pages.

1. Planning for differentiation in schemes of work/lesson plans

- The Group: Is it mixed-ability, an ability set or banded? What kind of prior knowledge and understanding might the pupils bring to the topic?
- The Approach: What approach will suit the teaching group? Define clear objectives which you want all pupils to achieve over a series of lessons.
- The Content: Consider the 'core' material (knowledge and understanding, skills and concepts), which will be for all pupils, then think of how this will be developed for different pupils. Consider a range of activities, including extension tasks for the more able.
- Resources: Look at potential resources. Are there books and other support materials accessible for different levels of ability and understanding?

2. Planning for differentiation through effective classroom organisation

- Classroom Layout: If there are to be different activities, how will these be organised?
- Equipment: Ensure that equipment and resources are accessible and well-labelled.
- Tasks: When preparing tasks or writing worksheets, focus on print size, layout, visual interest, illustrations and highlight key words. Use accessible language, explain key words and concepts. Make the lesson relevant to pupils' lives and provide opportunities for success and personal enjoyment.

3. Planning for differentiation through teaching styles and approaches

- Language: How will you explain and communicate the 'core' material to all pupils?
- Method: Use a good range of teaching methods. A mixture of individual and group work is helpful.
- Stimulus: Where there are different activities going on within a lesson, it is particularly important to bring the whole class together, certainly at the start and completion of a lesson.
- Support: Decide how pupils will be helped by you and any additional teacher.

4. Planning for differentiation through pupils' learning experiences

- Explain: Indicate to pupils the importance of the different activities so they appreciate all are valuable ways of learning. Outline the value of working individually, in pairs and in groups. Over time, vary the composition of the groups.
- Recording: Offer pupils or guide individuals into different ways of recording information such as note taking, flow diagrams, charts and use of word-processors.
- Assessment: Plan how the work will be assessed. Will it be on an individual or group basis? Will the criteria cover a range of activities?

Section 5.
PLANNING THE CURRICULUM

Effective and detailed planning is essential to the success of an RE department. This section explores strategies for broad planning and the development of schemes of work.

Stage 1:
Selection of material

Your syllabus needs to be based upon the local authority agreed syllabus, diocesan syllabus or the independent schools' syllabus. Make sure that each member of the department has a copy. The first stage is to break down the content of this syllabus into manageable units or modules. If the syllabus allows you a choice over which religions to study, think carefully about teacher expertise in the department, current resources and backgrounds of the pupils.

Stage 2:
Mapping the curriculum

Once you have decided which material you are going to cover in any key stage, you need to break down the material into individual teaching years. It is useful at this stage to 'map your curriculum' so that you can see at a glance which modules are going to be covered when. This map is also a useful tool to show to parents and governors who want to see an overview of the courses you are offering. When mapping out an RE curriculum you need to include material from your syllabus but you also need to bring to bear on this your own creativity and imagination to make the subject come alive and meet the individual needs of your pupils. You do not have to keep rigidly to the same wording as the syllabus you are adopting. Consider the following points when mapping your RE curriculum:

1. Use existing syllabus titles or design your own. It is best at this stage if they are descriptive and give a clear idea of the content of the course. You can use more imaginative titles later on when you present the course to pupils.
2. Make it clear on the map which religions you are offering for study.
3. Ensure that there is coherence and progression through the modules.
4. Check that there is a variety of modules across any given year - for example, one module studying a religion in depth; one which takes a thematic approach and another studying an ultimate question.
5. Indicate where end of module or termly tests are going to fall.

RE mapping allows you to keep a check on where you are going to be using your resources. For example, if you have three teachers teaching year 8 you can plan your modules so that the same resources can be used with different classes in different modules. Also, at key stages 4 & 5 an RE Map allows you to plan out examination courses. It helps to show how you are going to cover all the material in the two-year course. You can also plot on the times of coursework assignments.

The RE map could be described as a form of long-term planning. Each year group can have its own map and pupils can also have a copy so that they know what they are going to be studying throughout the year. The following page gives an example of one such map.

Example: KEY STAGE 3 MAP OF RE CURRICULUM

	Autumn Term	Spring Term	Summer Term
YEAR 7	**What is religion? Why study RE?** 1. Reasons for studying RE 2. Religion in the local community 3. Big questions which religion tries to answer 4. The impact of religion in the world	**Judaism and Christianity - Understanding the Bible. An introduction to the Bible as a library of books.** 1. To show the influence of the Bible on people today 2. To show how the Jewish Scriptures and the Christian Bible are used in Judaism and Christianity	**Christianity - The Life and Teaching of Jesus. This course enables pupils to look at the life of Jesus and his influence today.** 1. To describe important Christian beliefs related to Jesus (Incarnation, Atonement, Resurrection, Second Coming)
YEAR 8	**Judaism - Judaism as a world religion.** A study of the beliefs and practices of Judaism showing their impact and influence on individual Jewish lives and the world. To include a study of important historical events for the Jews - including the Holocaust	**A thematic study across a number of religions: Rites of Passage and special places.** 1. Life as a journey 2. Significant points on the journey 3. Birth & coming-of-age ceremonies 4. Marriage & funeral ceremonies	**Christianity - Key Christian Beliefs. A study of the Christian world view through its key beliefs.** Beliefs about: God, Creation, Humanity and Jesus including the meaning of his death and his Second Coming, Christian living and life after death
YEAR 9	**Buddhism - Buddhism as a world religion.** This course introduces pupils to the central teachings of Siddhartha Gautama, the Buddha 1. Three Refuges 2. The life of Siddhartha Gautama 3. Four Noble Truths 4. Eightfold Path	**Buddhism, Christianity, Judaism: The problem of suffering.** 1. Why people suffer 2. Natural and human-made suffering 3. Religious questions in the face of suffering 4. Evil and suffering 5. Buddhist response to suffering 6. The Holocaust - a case study 7. Jewish responses to suffering 8. Christian responses to suffering	**A thematic study across a number of religions: Faith affects action.** A study of how religious belief affects people's morality. Pupils will study the teaching of different religions on the following topics: 1. The family and close personal relationships 2. Sexual ethics 3. The environment and animal rights 4. War and peace

Example: SCHEME OF WORK FORMAT

TITLE OF UNIT:

RELIGIONS:

TIME (weeks / lessons):

Weeks / Lessons	Syllabus Reference: e.g. programme of study, attainment targets or end of key stage statements	General Learning Objectives	Content: Knowledge and Key Questions	Concepts Skills Attitudes	Activities Tasks (including homework)	Resources	Assessment Opportunities
1							
2							
3							
4							

Stage 3: Writing schemes of work

A scheme of work covers a module or unit of work from the RE map and puts flesh on it. There are a number of different formats which you can use for this but it is best to use a format that you find easy to work with. A good scheme of work is an ongoing planning document that should show progression within a topic. It needs to be written in advance and then updated as it is taught. For examination courses, the scheme breaks down a public examination syllabus into units of work to which you can attach coursework assignments. This stage could be defined as medium-term planning within the department's overall planning strategies.

A scheme of work can be for any period of time - from lessons to weeks. It should - usually - cover the following areas:

- key concepts;
- learning objectives;
- key questions;
- skills and attitudes;
- content;
- resources;
- teaching and learning methods;
- assessment opportunities;
- relationship to syllabus;
- homework activities.

One useful innovation is to make each scheme of work into a large poster for the wall so that all pupils can see the progression of the course. This will also allow pupils who have been absent for a lesson to know what topic they need to catch up on. By putting a copy of the scheme of work on the wall, pupils are given greater confidence about the direction their work is taking.

Stage 4: Individual lesson plans

While the scheme of work describes a unit of work over a number of lessons or weeks, the lesson plan describes just one lesson. It should be so detailed that if you were absent any colleague could pick up the plan and teach the lesson for you. Whilst the scheme of work might serve several teaching groups, the lesson plan is geared to one particular class. A lesson plan should provide:

- a descriptive title for the lesson;
- some specific short-term learning objectives;
- a link with previous lesson(s);
- an outline of content;
- an indication of where this lesson falls within a current scheme of work;
- details of the resources and materials required;
- key questions to start a discussion;
- a note on differentiation including ideas for extension work;
- a copy of any worksheet to be used;
- homework task(s);
- space for a short evaluation.

The preparation of lesson plans can be very time-consuming. Keeping lesson plans in a ring-binder together with the worksheets allows them to be recycled. It can help to divide the ring-binder into the different programmes of study you are following for each year. Photocopy good examples of pupils' work which can be used to inspire others if you repeat the course. Computers now provide an even better facility for storing your lesson plans so long as you have easy access to them. A sample lesson plan outline is provided below.

RELIGIOUS EDUCATION DEPARTMENT

Teacher	Class & Date

Subject of lesson

Context of lesson *(i.e. lesson 4 of 6 on Rites of Passage)*

show links with previous lessons

Learning Objectives

1.

2.

3.

Resources / materials necessary for the lesson

(e.g. textbook - indicate pages; worksheet(s); artefacts; materials for making things etc.)

Content of lesson	Key Questions	Tasks / Activities
(showing development)		*(showing differentiation - extension tasks etc.)*
		Homework: *(indicating when it is to be handed in)*

Evaluation

(Things which went well and things to change)

Classroom Activities

Classroom assignments can be many and varied - as the checklist below shows - but the most helpful type of assessment is criterion referenced. That means that the pupil understands that the mark or grade awarded is based on specific criteria - of which the pupil is aware. Examples of marked assignments (from another class) help pupils see what a particular grade is like. Below, is a checklist of the different kinds of activities that are appropriate for the RE classroom. It is important to provide variety when designing assignments.

Twenty-five classroom activities for RE

Activity	Examples
1. Essay writing	... either based on available resources or carried out under test conditions.
2. Researching topics	... using relevant resources, either in the department or library or at home.
3. Designing informative wallcharts, and posters	... using magazines, newspapers and media quotations.
4. Designing factsheets	... either for same age pupils or for a younger group.
5. Writing a biographical sketch of a religious figure	... to bring out the turning points in his or her life. Can be presented as 'This is your life'!
6. Writing an appreciation of the life of a person	... highlighting personal beliefs, values and achievements.
7. Compiling a travel guide or brochure	... for a place of specific religious interest.
8. Writing a diary	... to record thoughts or to empathise with a person studied.
9. Writing a playscript	... turning prose or stories into play form.
10. Writing eye-witness accounts	... it is possible to use desktop publishing to create authentic materials and develop IT skills.
11. Writing newspaper articles	... the same opportunities as above.
12. Writing advertising features	... to sell a particularly unpopular belief or promote a religious idea.
13. Letter writing	... to a penfriend explaining a religious custom or after a bereavement, or to newspapers.
14. Preparing a school assembly	... relating to a topic studied in class.
15. Writing a review of a film, television programme or book	... a religious programme or one that is clearly not religious in its approach.
16. Newspaper study	... comparing newspaper articles with an examination of their bias.
17. Writing and delivering a speech	... or sermon.
18. Designing a meal menu	... appropriate to a particular faith tradition.
19. Inventing a festival	... to celebrate a religious belief or idea.
20. Designing a building	... to accommodate a religious faith tradition.

21. Writing a manifesto	... summarising the main issues in a subject..
22. Taking part in debates	... writing speeches or arguments for a debate.
23. Interviewing	... someone on their beliefs and values.
24. Questionnaires	... devised and appropriate conclusions drawn.
25. Writing devotional material	... a prayer, a meditation.

Homework

Homework is a valuable tool for extending the amount of time pupils spend on religious education. If it is carefully planned, it can produce creative pieces of work; stimulate family interest in the subject; and enable pupils to become individually engaged in personal research. If homework is to achieve these goals the following issues need to be taken into consideration.

The RE department needs to have its own homework policy which draws on that of the school's. The policy should provide information on when homework should be set and what happens if pupils hand it in late or fail to complete it. This will ensure that all pupils are treated in the same way. The homework policy needs to be communicated to pupils and parents. A copy of it could be attached to the inside cover of the pupils' exercise books. In order that homework should be a purposeful activity, it should be carefully planned and given the same amount of preparation time as classwork tasks. It is not a good idea for pupils to be given classwork to 'finish off' since this will mean that the more able pupils will often find themselves with little, if anything, to do. If homework tasks are planned carefully the pupil's interest can be caught. Imaginative tasks can encourage pupils to spend considerable time on RE. Finally, if research tasks are set, the teacher needs to ensure that adequate resources are available.

Homework in RE

Homework can be used to:

- extend and develop classwork;
- test the pupils' understanding of a lesson;
- raise interest in a new topic;
- extend RE into the world at large - for example, by asking pupils to collect material from newspapers or from television programmes, you are making links with their 'everyday' world and reinforcing the impression that RE has much to do with everyday life.

If the school library can be used, it is a good idea to talk to the librarian in advance so that books can be ordered and displays arranged. It is important to recognise that some pupils will not have access to supporting material at home. Some departments produce information booklets consisting of photocopiable sheets to remedy this.

When setting homework think about the end product. How will it be marked? As an example, giving your pupils an essay might be an easy thing for you to set but you will have to spend a disproportionate amount of time marking it. Leave enough time at the end of the lesson for all pupils to write the instructions down. In order to set tasks which produce high quality work you may need to spend five or ten minutes in class setting up the topic perhaps by a class brainstorm on how to approach a homework topic. Sometimes it is helpful to show pupils an example of the finished product in order to inspire and encourage them.

Homework tasks should be varied and utilise resources which are not so readily available in the classroom. Research tasks, questionnaires, interviews with parents, television and book reviews are activities that lend themselves to homework. The department can usefully start to collect a pool of homework topics on specific modules of work in addition to collecting together a portfolio of examples of pupils' work which can be used to inspire future pupils.

Homework Activities in RE

The following are interesting for pupils and keep your marking to a minimum:

- questionnaires for other pupils, friends and relations;
- a newspaper search on a given topic;
- preparing a piece of work for a wall display;
- television watching such as viewing a soap opera and exploring the current moral issues involved or a review of the news on a given day in order to collect material on a topic such as suffering;
- travel research to find background information on a country with religious significance such as Israel or India;
- reading fiction - many novels can be used as background material to a course;
- collecting pictures for use in a collage.

Homework marks should be accurately recorded and distinguishable from classwork, so that you can see where pupils' strengths lie. It is important to mark homework promptly and hand books back by the next lesson. There is plenty of evidence that unmarked homework demotivates pupils. When returning homework to pupils, try to spend a few minutes commenting on the work they have produced. This shows that you are taking homework seriously. Finally, make homework interesting, relevant and fun in order to get the best results. It then becomes a very effective way of extending the amount of time pupils spend on RE and also raises their motivation for the subject.

The RE Handbook

While there is no legal requirement that an RE department should have a handbook, all curriculum areas in the school are now expected to produce documentation, much of which is required for OFSTED inspection. The advice that follows is designed for teachers who are either compiling documentation from the start or revising an existing document. A handbook is the chance to reflect your own vision of the RE department. Even if the school has adopted a particular format and guidelines it should be possible to add relevant material as you feel is appropriate. Before you start writing, you need to consider the following:

1. **Audience:** Create your documentation for a wide audience. Staff within your own school, inspectors, advisers, governors, parents and student teachers may request to view your handbook. Not all of the readers will be teachers or experts.

2. **Style:** Some of your readers will be familiar with the terminology associated with religious education but many others will not. Make your documentation clear and readable for lay-people and explain terms where appropriate.

3. **Format:** The most popular format is the ring-binder. It has the advantage that pages can be extracted easily and updating is not a problem. However, it is wise to avoid using page numbers so that if you update and extend particular sections there is no difficulty in renumbering pages. Instead, use a clear index, and units or chapters broken down into sections and sub-sections. Remember, the handbook is a working document and is on-going.

4. **Presentation:** To create the best possible impression of the department include different styles and methods of presentation. Use diagrams and flow charts. In addition to the various policies, include some photographs showing different aspects of RE or include a brief section showing some samples of pupils' work. A summary of evaluative comments from pupils about their views on RE can bring a document to life very effectively.

Other school documents

There should be an entry about RE in the school prospectus which should be updated as necessary. There may well be other school documents including a year 9 options booklet and years 12 & 13 choice booklets where you will have the opportunity to describe the RE courses available.

Areas to include in an RE Department Handbook

Aims and Objectives

Policy Statements: Equal Opportunities; Health & Safety; Discipline and Behaviour; Spiritual, Moral, Social and Cultural Development; Marking; Assessing, Recording and Reporting; Homework.

Staffing Information: Members of the department, teaching experience, specific responsibilities. Head of department job description.

A map of RE provision including:

1. Time allocation for each year group as a percentage of whole curriculum, organisation of teaching groups - mixed-ability, banded or in sets.
2. Year by year description of objectives, content, approaches, religions studied, opportunities to show evidence of progression and assessment.
3. Examination courses: At GCSE, AS and A Level.

Teaching and learning:

1. Statement on teaching and learning styles and strategies including how RE meets the needs of pupils of all abilities.
2. Description of skills and attitudes promoted.
3. Analysis of external examination results.

Links:

1. with faith communities through visits and visitors;
2. with cross-curricular skills/themes/dimensions;
3. to information technology.

Departmental issues:

1. Accommodation and facilities;
2. Resources;
3. Budget and funding;
4. Departmental meetings - agendas and minutes;
5. Departmental Development Plan;
6. INSET profiles of staff.

Other documents:

1. Records of formal visits to RE department by external bodies such as OFSTED inspection and local education authority monitoring.

Section 6.
USING RESOURCES

At its heart, religious education is the exploration of living faiths in the classroom. The resources teachers use should aim, in as far as it is possible, to bring these faiths alive to the pupils. Some resources are better at doing this than others. This section provides information about resources and offers some suggestions on how to use them.

When considering which resources to buy and use, three overriding points are worth considering. Firstly, it is important to have a range of resources for each religion including videos, artefacts, slides and books and to catalogue them in an accessible way - perhaps on a word-processor. Secondly, care should be taken in how resources are stored. Some departments use large cardboard boxes - one for each major religion. And, finally, many resources can be created and made by the RE department, thus cutting down their cost.

1 Religious Artefacts

A religious artefact is an object which is used by religious people in practising their faith. Many are associated with worship. The use of religious artefacts can bring pupils into contact with a living faith. Some artefacts are special to adherents because they believe that the divine communicates with them through it, such as holy books, while others are used for practical reasons, such as incense holders.

It should never be forgotten that artefacts have religious significance. For this reason, the RE department needs to have a clear policy on how artefacts should be used and under what criteria they are collected. Pupils should also be taught how faith communities respect them and how to show respect for them themselves. For example, pupils should not be allowed to touch a Qur'an before washing their hands while a Buddha rupa must not be left on the floor and should be kept in a high position above the heads of people. One way of encouraging enquiry and interest is to present an artefact in a bag so that pupils can't actually see it. Pupils should be encouraged to feel the artefact and suggest what it is and what it is used for. Encouraging pupils to feel artefacts in this way can bring religion alive and create interest.

Obtaining artefacts

There are a number of possible sources for artefacts. Faith communities can be approached and pupils and parents may have religious items which they use in worship at home and which they would be willing to bring in and share with the class. There are also a number of specialist religious shops in major towns and cities which sell religious artefacts and specialist bookshops may stock a limited range. The *Resource Guide* includes details of mail-order services. Finally, it may be worth asking a Parent-School Association or an educational trust to support the purchase of artefacts.

Why use religious artefacts?

The sensitive use of artefacts can:

- bring religions to life and bring pupils into closer contact with a religious tradition;
- stimulate deeper understanding of other peoples' religious expression;
- provide information about a faith;
- act as stimuli for discussion, creative writing or story telling;
- invite pupils to ask questions. What is it? What is it used for? Why is it important to believers?
- encourage personal reflection;
- communicate spiritual truths in ways which a text book does not;
- be preparation for a visit to a place of worship;
- introduce a religion or a topic within a religion;
- develop observation skills in preparation for watching a video - objects to spot during the video;
- aid memory;
- be good preparation for a museum visit;
- be an aid to revision;
- encourage respect and help develop empathy;
- appeal to the senses;
- help pupils to feel affirmed in their faith.

Collections of artefacts

Artefacts can be collected to support the study of each principal faith. They should be stored in a safe place. A lockable glass cabinet is ideal. They can then be taken out and used in displays together with books, posters and other resources. The *Resource Guide* offers suggestions as to what a department might like to collect from each religion. It is important to underline that a collection need not be expensive and that some artefacts can be made in the classroom or as a homework activity. Even some types of food can be used as artefacts. Food plays an important role in many religions and has a strong appeal to the senses.

Introducing artefacts

It is also important to let the artefacts speak for themselves. Pupils should be encouraged to ask questions of the artefact. For example, you could provide them with the following stimulus questions: What is it used for? Which religion is it used in? How can you tell? Is the artefact symbolic? If so, what do you think it means? Once a group of pupils have discussed an artefact, they can be encouraged to find out the answers to their questions. They can then write up their findings in the form of information cards which can be used in a display using a number of artefacts. Alternatively, once pupils have found out about the artefact they can give a presentation to the rest of the class.

2 Textbooks

Textbooks need to be selected and used with care. When deciding on which textbook to use, the first question to answer is how suitable the book is for use in the school and how far it meets the needs of the pupils you are buying it for. You then have to ask yourself if the reading level is appropriate for the needs of your pupils, will any illustrations and photographs invite them to use it and are the activities sufficiently differentiated so that some are appropriate for both the least and the most able. You also have to ask if the activities enable pupils to learn both about, and from, the faith and are sufficiently varied. The final question to consider is how far the text meets the requirements of your syllabus. It is worth inquiring whether there is a photocopiable teacher's manual to go with the book which can be useful for extension and homework activities.

In addition to commercial textbooks, it may be worthwhile producing your own 'in house' materials. These can have the advantage of meeting your direct needs. However, it is important to produce booklets of a high standard. Pupils are entitled to expect good quality material to work with. Also, great care must be taken when producing your own booklets not to infringe an author's or publisher's copyright.

A good textbook has many uses. It can stand as a class set and provide the basis for a school course, look good on display and be a useful source of pictures. It can also support individual pupils who are carrying out research for coursework.

3 Videotapes

If used correctly videos can create atmosphere, bring a religion to life and make links with everyday life. They can show the relevance of religion to peoples' lives. With creative planning, teachers can use a wide range of video material within the classroom. Some films have specific religious content such as the series, *Jesus of Nazareth*. Other films contain material which explore themes pertinent to the RE classroom. For example, the film *Dead Poets Society* explores important themes about life. *National Geographic* films about nature are very useful, for example, in supporting work on creation.

Different ways to use videotapes

Videotapes should not be used solely to entertain. So, in the RE classroom:-

- prepare pupils and focus their attention by asking them to look out for specific things;
- use small extracts to focus pupils' minds;
- where appropriate, present a worksheet to accompany the video. If it is a short extract, it may be helpful to watch it once before looking at the worksheet;
- pause the video at key points to give pupils a chance to ask questions and seek clarification;
- introduce the tape by showing pupils any artefacts which will appear in it;
- ask pupils to write their own video review - as a critic for an RE magazine;
- turn down the sound commentary and ask pupils to devise their own;
- use videotape to review a topic for revision purposes.

---

4 Visits

Visits are an important part of the RE department's work. The value of a visit is that it can bring pupils into contact with living faiths, encourage pupils to ask questions and increase the amount of time pupils are involved in RE. Visits are suitable for all abilities and pupils can gain from a well-planned visit at many different levels. Visits appeal to the senses and give pupils a 'feel' for the religion. It is also worth noting how visits involve parents and guardians at home and can add prestige and popularity to the department because they promote interest and provide opportunities for follow-up research work.

It is not always easy to make contacts when you want to arrange a visit. However, introductions can come through a local adviser or a college of higher education RE department and many towns have a round table of religions or a multicultural centre which will provide names. Also, local networks of teachers are invariably helpful since other colleagues have tried and tested different places to visit.

Any visit has to be well-planned and clearly structured. Visits should arise naturally out of the programme of study you are following and the headteacher must have given permission after being informed well in advance. It is also advisable to give advance warning of visits to other colleagues and to follow school guidelines carefully. If at all possible, visit the places you intend to go to beforehand and make sure that any verbal arrangements you have made are confirmed in writing.

Making visits a success - best practice

1. **Send a letter to parents.** Teachers of RE have minimal opportunities to raise their subject with parents. Use this letter to inform parents about more than the timetable and the cost. Present an itinerary, give background information about the religion and link the visit to work done in school. Explain how the visit is going to be used and set objectives so that the pupils know in advance that the visit is full of purpose.

2. **Invite a member of the senior management team, an interested parent or parents and a governor to come on the trip with you.** It is good marketing to educate your supporters! The aims of the day should also be publicised to other pupils and teachers.

3. **Use the lesson(s) before the visit to provide necessary background.** Make sure that pupils are aware of what to look for and are encouraged to bring cameras.

4. **Clarify the school's behaviour policy.** Do you need to add to it?

5. **Videotape of your visit.** This is very useful for showing on open evening.

6. **Ensure that the pupils write thank you letters** to all those involved in arranging the visits.

7. **After the visit, capitalise upon it.** Make a display of photographs, pupils' work and artefacts to go in a prominent position in the school for staff and visitors to see.

5 Visitors

A visitor to the department brings specialist skills and expertise. As a member of a faith community a visitor has first-hand experience and knowledge to share. Visitors can also bring existing teaching materials to life, provide links with living faith traditions, relate religion to life and act as a resource for pupils' questionings.

Using visitors entails time and planning. In order to ensure that they are used to their best effect it is essential for the school and the classes to be well-prepared. Always seek the permission of the headteacher in advance.

Visitors - a guide

1   Make sure that your visitors are suitable. Meet them beforehand and discuss what they plan to do. If possible, see them working in another school with young people. Agree expenses. Colleagues from other schools can be a useful resource for names, as can a local authority RE advisor or inspector.

2   Once you have found a visitor, brief him or her carefully. During this meeting mention the size of the class and age range of pupils, discuss the religious and cultural mix of the group and explain the educational context of the classroom. Show him or her the work which the class has been doing. For all visitors who are going to engage with pupils, discuss the content of what they are to say in specific terms, including how long you want them to speak for and any activities which the visitor may wish to do. Explain the format the lesson will take and warn against activities which may compromise pupils. Ask about any materials they will need such as a projector or video-recorder. If there is going to be a follow-up session, say what form this is going to take - for example, a worksheet, discussion topic, research or a visit to a place of worship. Finally, ask how they would like to be introduced.

3   Follow-up this meeting with a formal invitation confirming the date, time and contents of the lesson. Enclose a map of the school with directions and information about car parking. Make sure that you provide a contact telephone number in case of emergencies. It is advisable to provide a home telephone number where they can contact you the evening before in case they have questions needing clarification.

4   Before the visit, prepare your class. Ask them to write down any questions which they would like to ask the visitor and arrange for somebody to meet him or her. At the beginning of the lesson, introduce the visitor, but don't pre-empt what they are going to say or do.

5   After the visit offer refreshments. This provides an important opportunity for feedback and debriefing as well as for thanks. Follow up the visit with a letter expressing thanks and providing any positive feedback. The pupils themselves could write letters of thanks and include examples of the work which followed the visit. Care needs to be taken, however, not to give positive feedback on a disastrous visit! Some visitors may take this as encouragement to repeat the performance in other schools.

---

6 Information Technology

Some RE teachers find it a challenge to develop the use of IT within their lessons because of a lack of equipment within the RE department or difficulties in booking the main computing facilities. Also, with one lesson a week some teachers have decided that they cannot afford the time to focus on IT. However, RE must not fall behind other subjects. RE teachers should be on the look out for relevant software and aim to use information technology as a tool which can bring its own opportunities and engage pupils in new and interesting ways.

Information technology (IT) capability is characterised by an ability to use effectively IT tools and information sources to analyse, process and present information, and to model, measure and control external events. This involves:

- using information sources and information technology tools to solve problems;
- using information technology tools and information sources such as computer systems and software packages, to support learning in a variety of contexts;
- understanding the implications of information technology for working life and society.

(National Curriculum Order for Information Technology, SCAA, 1995)

Ways in which information technology can be used in the RE department

1. **Encourage the use of word-processing programmes:** to produce both draft and finished classwork, homework and coursework.

2. **Use desktop-publishing (DTP):** to link text and graphics together for producing information sheets, newspaper tasks and wall displays. Add a **scanner** so that pupils can incorporate photographs.

3. **Use tape and video-recorders:** to interview members of faith traditions or to produce sound tracks to accompany a slide show or presentation.

4. **Use colour acetates:** to make use of photographs that pupils have taken in a class presentation or use acetates of famous paintings to trace a religious theme.

5. **Use CD ROM's:** to provide pupils with access to vast amounts of information, including text, sound, pictures and graphics.

6. **Use the Internet:** to allow pupils to contact religious organisations as well as other schools which are working on similar projects.

One way to unravel the IT curriculum, is to see how the skills, knowledge and understanding of information technology can be organised into the following strands: monitoring, controlling, modelling, and communicating and handling information. This implies that, in RE, pupils should therefore be given opportunities to access and collect information, communicate their ideas using information technology, analyse data and consider some of the social, economic, ethical and moral issues raised by information technology.

7 Photographs and Pictures

It is important that pictures work for you in the classroom. They are generally underused and have many more uses than the merely illustrative. Photographs and pictures can be collected from a wide range of sources. These include specialist packs, newspapers and colour supplements, nature magazines, textbooks, travel books, postcards, travel brochures and personal photographs. It is well worth visiting discount book shops which often have travel books at reduced prices. Wallcharts can also be a valuable way to combine pictures and information.

Activities using photographs and pictures

Questions

What can you see and what do you notice?
Why are people behaving in this way?
Which part of a story does it illustrate?
What is this person thinking and feeling?
What things matter to the people in the photograph or picture? How can you tell?
What would you like to ask these people?
What are you thinking as you look at the pictures? Write down all the words and phrases that come to mind.
What would you do if you walked into the situation shown in the photograph?
Who do you identify with?

Labelling the images

Provide a title which brings out the meaning of a picture.
Write your own caption to a photograph in which you try to describe the feelings behind the faces.
Write a postcard home having just seen the picture on holiday. How would you describe it? What do you think the artist is trying to say? What feelings come to mind when you look at it?
Look at the picture. If it could speak what would it say?

Comparing the images

How are these pictures the same? How are they different?
Why do different artists paint the same scene in completely different ways? What is their message?

These images can be used with individual pupils or superimposed onto transparencies. Many film-processing shops have the capacity to produce colour acetates from photographs or pictures and these are worth collecting in folders dedicated to a particular religion or filed by theme. They can then be stored in resource boxes for use by pupils alongside individual copies of books, artefacts and information sheets for individual or group research.

8 Stories

Nobody, but nobody, was paying attention to the Indian Prime Minister. Her arguments were sound and her ideas compelling but her speech was falling on stony ground. No one was taking any interest. She paused. 'Once upon a time', she said, starting again. Suddenly everyone was quiet, everyone was listening. 'Once upon a time, the Prime Minister of India went for a walk with a swallow and an eel'. She had them all now, she knew, in the palm of her hand.

(Inside Stories, Wood A & Richardson R, Trentham, 1992)

As the Indian Prime Minister realised, those simple four words have a haunting effect. People sit up and take notice. This applies as much to pupils in years 12 and 13 as to younger pupils. They love stories and, when told well, they are a rich resource for use in RE. If used well, they speak directly to the heart of the listeners and reveal their own meaning. All the great religious teachers have known this. For example, Jesus rarely explained his parables, he did not need to. A parable uses a familiar everyday incident as a means of encountering a deeper truth. The storyteller uses the known and familiar in order to disclose the unacknowledged or previously avoided. Stories like this have a power of their own to enlighten the heart. There are two main types of story for use in RE: religious stories which arise out of the faith tradition, and everyday stories.

> Someone said to an Eastern mystic:
> 'You relate stories, but you do not tell us how to understand them'.
> He said:
> 'How would you like it if the man from whom you bought fruit consumed it before your eyes, leaving only the skin?'
>
> *(100 Readings for Assembly, Idries Shah, Heinemann, 1993)*

All religions have a wealth of stories. They are used to instruct, to inform, to encourage, to reprimand, to provide guidance, give warnings and, at times, to simply entertain. They are a means by which shared values and meanings are transmitted down the ages. In addition, it could be said that each religion has its own single major story. This is its unique vision of the world, its distinctive account of where the world came from, where it is going and its unique vision of the good life. This story provides the structure of the religion in a highly simplified form. Pupils need to be introduced to these distinctive stories in order to understand each religion. As Wood and Richardson argue, 'If you wish to get to know a religious tradition better, then the most valuable thing for you to do is to go inside the tradition's stories and its story'.

Everyday stories are important because people have their own personal stories and biographies. There is a certain mystery to these stories, since they are not yet complete. People retell their stories in order to make sense of their lives, to draw together the threads of their story to discover the meaning. Pupils enjoy learning about the life stories of others; famous people, people in newspapers and especially their teachers! They love the personal anecdote, especially if it is amusing. Meanings are much easier to grasp if they are embodied in a personal story. However, it is easier to discover the meaning of other people's stories than of one's own:

'How do I attain wisdom?' the young man asked.
'You get wisdom,' replied the teacher, 'by listening to your own story. You are a book, and you have to read and study the book which is you'.
The young man looked puzzled. 'And it's difficult, very difficult', continued the teacher, 'because every day there's a new page, and every moment there's a new word, in the book which is you'.

Religious teachers and spiritual guides have recognised this down the ages. They call people to live 'the examined life', a call to reflection and personal examination. By encouraging pupils to acts of mental self-examination, teachers can promote their spiritual development. In this, stories become a vehicle of revelation.

Making stories a success

The best stories:

- are told rather than read and are unfolded bit by bit;
- put pupils at ease. It is for good reasons that storytellers have traditionally started by using the phrase, 'Are you sitting comfortably...';
- encourage pupils to get inside the story and visualise the events being described - the use of artefacts can aid this process;
- make links with our deepest selves. For example, in the story of religious figures pupils can be encouraged to identify aspects of themselves;
- rarely need a commentary;
- encourage pupils to interrogate their meaning and raise questions about them.

Section 7.
ASSESSMENT, RECORDING AND REPORTING

This section sets out guidelines for assessment, recording and reporting in the RE department including advice on policies and marking.

Policies

Most schools now accept assessment as an integral part of the teaching and learning process. Pupils' progress in RE, like that in any other subject, must be assessed. Without regular assessment, the subject lacks rigour and status and pupils are unclear about how to make progress. However, it must be remembered that pupils' personal beliefs are not being assessed, recorded or reported. This is not always understood by those outside the RE world. So, RE teachers need to be quite clear about why, and what, they are assessing when they come to write their departmental policies.

Since RE is not part of the national curriculum, there are no national guidelines (produced by SCAA, for example) relating to assessment in RE. However, two publications have been particularly influential. These are *Forms of Assessment in RE* (FARE Project, 1991) and *Assessment, Recording and Reporting in RE* (Westhill RE Centre, 1991). Since these documents were produced, many local authorities, SACREs and dioceses have devised similar guidance.

There are a number of policy issues to consider in relation to assessment, recording and reporting in RE. Where a school has a general policy on assessing, recording and reporting, it is necessary to find out to what extent the RE department is expected to follow this guidance. Also, where the RE department is part of a bigger faculty such as humanities, there may be a faculty policy on assessing, recording and reporting which must be adopted. In other cases, any policy or system devised by the RE department must be clear and reasonably simple. It needs to be understood by colleagues, pupils and parents. Where a policy already exists, it is important to check on how it is operating and to ask whether it can be improved within a cycle of regular review. The policy should always relate back to the RE syllabus. The latter will probably set out the criteria for assessment in terms of factual knowledge and understanding, and pupils' skills in responding to and evaluating material.

Assessment

In discussing assessment, it is important to recognise that the term can be interpreted in several ways. Taken in its broadest sense, it would be true to say that teachers are continually assessing pupils' abilities in a variety of ways. Sometimes this will be done informally in the way, for example, that a teacher listens to group or class discussions or comments on written work as he or she moves around the classroom. Pupils may not even be aware that an assessment is taking place and the teacher may, or may not, decide to record this kind of assessment. However, assessment can also be a more formal exercise where the teacher has planned specific opportunities into a scheme of work. Pupils can be well aware of the assessment activity and the teacher can explain the criteria for the assessment showing what the pupil is being asked to demonstrate in terms of knowledge, understanding or evaluation.

Good assessment builds on self-knowledge, giving pupils regular opportunities to reflect on how they are doing. It has to be positive in that it should focus on what pupils know, understand and can do. It should celebrate strengths. The use of merits, RE award stickers, special prizes, letters home, wall displays and praise in school bulletins are ways to make this happen.

Assessment has to be both formative and summative. Formative assessment is on-going, enabling the teacher to identify areas of strength and weakness for each pupil and providing targets for future learning. Summative assessment will give a summary of a pupil's progress at the end of each unit of work or at the end of a term, a year or a key stage. It will be evaluative in that it is set against prescribed criteria. Worth mentioning in this context is the need to look at samples of pupils' work regularly and carry out a moderation exercise. This helps to ensure that marking of assessed work is consistent across a year group and department. A later section in this chapter shows how work that has been the focus of moderation can be built into a portfolio.

Marking

Marking is extremely important to the teaching and learning process and has to be seen as an integral part of curriculum planning rather than an addition to it. As schemes of work are developed, the RE teacher needs to consider how many pieces of work or assignments will be formally assessed. This will, of course, depend on the length of the unit of work but there must be regular and scheduled opportunities for assessment. Marking can take a range of forms ranging from grades, percentages or comments to a brief tick to indicate the teacher has noted and approved the piece of work. RE staff generally teach a large number of classes which places constraints on marking. It is best for the department to decide how often exercise books or folders will be marked in each year group. It may not be possible to mark and assess every pupil's work every week and once a fortnight may be more realistic. It is important to devise a system that is manageable.

The department needs to consider the most useful method of marking particular types of work according to the demands of the school assessment system, the time available to the teacher and the needs of individual pupils. Perhaps the most effective marking is that which is done with the pupil present. However, this practice can be unrealistic in many cases. Marking should give clear feedback to pupils on how they are progressing. In this context, teachers have to train pupils to look at and understand teachers' comments and assessment grades. Peer assessment can also work well in RE where pupils assess each other within a group and, similarly, self-assessment can also be productive.

The teachers in the RE department have to decide what their marking will actually entail. For example, will they merely be concerned with RE knowledge, understanding and evaluation or will grammatical and spelling errors be corrected. It is important to relate such discussions to whole-school policies and make a departmental decision so that the approach adopted is consistent.

Once the RE department has agreed the policy then it needs to be communicated to pupils and parents. The best way of doing this is by explaining the marking system on a printed sheet which can be stuck inside the front cover of each pupil's exercise book. In addition, it can be explained by means of a poster in the classroom. Some schools use a system of grades and numbers when formally assessing a piece of work. These grades and numbers will usually focus on Attainment (what the pupil can do in terms of specified criteria) and Effort (how much enthusiasm, care and interest has been put in).

Why mark books regularly?

Detailed, periodic marking and reporting:

- gives feedback on progress;
- can encourage, guide and motivate pupils;
- monitors progress;
- recognises completion;
- gives individual advice;
- recognises effort;
- develops realistic pupil self-evaluation;
- can counsel;
- can identify particular learning needs and correct errors;
- can initiate a dialogue;
- can contribute to a record of achievement;
- enables the teacher to plan and differentiate more effectively;
- helps the teacher to evaluate teaching and resources;
- enlightens different audiences - pupils, colleagues, parents, employers.

Attainment	Effort	Attainment	Effort
A	1	D	4
B	2	E	5
C	3		

An example like the one above can be expanded with descriptive statements to show what each grade means. Also, the criteria for attainment can be made to relate to an examination syllabus. Accompanying written comments are most valuable where they are specific, enabling the pupil to achieve a particular target in the future.

Recording in RE

The following suggestions for how to record pupils' achievements in RE will have to be placed alongside school arrangements and any required by the chosen RE syllabus. It is worth underlining that if a school is following a clearly defined syllabus and related schemes of work across a year group, then there should be no need for each teacher to record what has been taught. What is being discussed here is how to record what pupils have achieved.

Deciding on how much should be recorded is up to the teacher. Obviously, it is important to have several sources of evidence through formal and informal assessment procedures but an RE teacher does not need to be recording notes every minute of every RE lesson. Any system must be workable and administration should be kept to a minimum. Consideration needs to be given as to how much and what kind of information should be passed onto other teachers. Any pass-on records must be clear and easy to interpret.

Grades

There are a number of different elements in the recording process. The most obvious are the results of individual, formally assessed tasks. Each term teachers will set some tasks to be formally assessed in line with the department's assessment policy. Each task will have specific criteria in relation to marking and these may well be related to curriculum attainment targets. The teacher awards a grade or a number depending on the system in operation and records this in a mark-book.

Comments

The second element in a record is teacher comments and observations. These derive from situations where assessment can be carried out less formally. For example, there will be occasions in lessons when pupils are working in groups with perhaps a spokesperson and a secretary. The rest of the group will contribute to the discussion. As the teacher moves around the groups, it will be possible to collect evidence about how individuals are contributing. Some will show insight, knowledge and understanding. Others will demonstrate effective listening skills. These contributions cannot so easily be graded and a teacher comment is far more effective. This is where it could be helpful to adapt a mark-book using perhaps two pages for a class and enabling a bigger space to be used for each pupil. A brief comment could be noted. In one lesson, a teacher will not be attempting to make notes on all pupils but over the course of a term or year, this will be possible.

Profiles

The third element is the comments made by pupils themselves and pupil profiles. These are very popular in some schools. Basically, a profile is a standard form designed by the department and given to pupils to fill in at the end of a unit of work or periodically. Although feedback from pupils can be invaluable, the advice here is that such forms should be used in moderation. Using profiles too frequently and across a number of curriculum subjects can mean that pupils get bored with filling them in and do not always take them seriously. They can also be time-consuming to produce and may not be sufficiently analysed by busy teachers. Where they are introduced, the key question to ask is how the pupils' comments can help to target their future learning. At its simplest, will their comments assist in future lesson planning? The best pupil profiles are attractively designed perhaps using appropriate religious symbols or words and are simple and clear to the reader. They aim for responses that specifically relate to RE content and approach. These kinds of questions are preferable to more general ones like: Did you hand your homework in on time? Did you bring the right equipment to lessons? Did you work hard? However, that is not to say that these sorts of questions could not be used in some situations.

Subject Portfolios

Finally, many primary schools have recently developed a subject portfolio for each subject to show the current standards followed by the school in particular areas. Secondary schools are now starting to see the advantages of following this system. Basically, a portfolio is an ongoing collection of pupils' work. It is not intended to be a huge sample but, instead, includes representative pieces of work, not necessarily from each taught topic nor from every class in a year group. An RE portfolio can contain a range of types of work including written material, artefacts, video films, audiotapes, posters, leaflets and photographs taken by pupils. A portfolio is very useful for inspection purposes (though it is not a requirement) and can show pupils and parents the achievements of pupils in RE through a range of tasks and activities. It should be updated on an annual basis.

Questions to ask in pupil self-assessment

- What did you learn from this module that you did not know before?

- What things did you find difficult to understand?

- Was there any particular activity or resource (video, pictures, books) that you found particularly helpful and enjoyable?

- Could you suggest any improvements to the teaching of this module?

Reporting RE

Reporting is the next stage on from recording. Teachers will have gathered a range of evidence about each pupil and the task here is to summarise that evidence into a report outlining individual progress and development. State schools are legally required to report to parents annually on progress in all subjects, including RE. Other schools will have similar arrangements. More frequent reporting to parents is also commonplace. Progress in RE has to be seen in terms of gains in knowledge, understanding of religion and the associated skills and concepts. The precise 'breakdown' of these areas will be as set out in the syllabus or guidelines which the school is following but the details will probably include the following:

1 Programmes of study - what pupils should be taught;
2 Attainment targets - the expected standards of performance;
3 End of year or end of key stage attainment statements - what pupils are expected to know, understand and can do;
   or
4 Level descriptions or end of key stage descriptions - a description of standards expected of the majority of pupils.

A pupil's progress will be reported against these markers. Some schools have a computer program containing a bank of statements to be used in the reporting process. Critics would claim that it is difficult to get a sense of warmth and individualisation using a bank of prepared statements. However, if the program has an extensive statement bank and teachers can add comments as appropriate, this can be an   effective   system.

School report formats vary and RE teachers will have to include whatever details the requirements specify. Some schools include a range of sections on the annual summative report which could include a statement of the topics covered in RE throughout the year and a pupil comment alongside the teachers. Particular achievements can, of course, be highlighted but the key question a teacher should ask is does this report summarise the pupil's progress in RE during the school year. Many schools have their own records of achievement that pupils take with them when they leave. Included in these would be a final report. Where schools have devised an RE Certificate for years 10 and 11 as part of a non-examination RE course, this too can be placed in the record of achievement folder.

Section 8.
EXAMINATIONS

Examinations, school-based and external, are a necessary part of the RE department and, unlike in other subject areas, their establishment can be challenging. This section reviews good practice in both areas.

Internal Examinations

Almost all schools hold internal examinations at the end of each year. Some hold additional tests throughout the year. All these examinations form part of the school's assessment policy and it is important to ensure that your examinations are compatible with this document. Sometimes, the school assessment policy will provide clear guidelines on how examinations should be written. In other schools, each department will be given a certain amount of flexibility. If your school does not hold internal examinations, this does not mean that you cannot organise your own departmental tests which will contribute to a grade.

The first priority is to plan well in advance and be clear about what you want as a department. In establishing this, consider the aim of the examination. Is it to test all or only part of the course? If it is a skill based test, why not ask pupils to apply what they have learnt to a new situation so that they have to 'think on their feet'. You also need to think about the style of the test and the type of questions to set. Remember that multiple choice questions may be easy to mark but may not tell you what you need to know. A useful inset exercise is to compile a database of different genre of questions by reading through different textbooks and old examinations papers.

Meet together with colleagues to discuss the format of the examinations and to brainstorm questions you could ask. Include student teachers in this process - they could also be encouraged to design part of an examination paper as one of their projects. Inform pupils well in advance of the subjects and topics which will be covered. If pupils know that they will be tested on certain topics, they will usually put more effort into their class and homework. Do not make the content of internal examinations a complete secret. Inform pupils of the type of questions and the format in which they will appear. Give pupils hints on how to revise. Even provide a revision sheet which could be in the form of a 'fill-in-the-gaps' worksheet which you can go through with the class in the previous lesson. As an integral part of this process provide adequate revision of skills. For example, assist pupils with essay writing skills and present them with model answers. Remember to make examination papers interesting. Use relevant newspaper articles discussing religious, spiritual and moral issues and use pictures and diagrams as stimuli - but ensure that they photocopy well!

There are two further issues for the department to decide its policy on. The first is the handing back of examination papers. Where this is done, it is important to comment on the examination and sometimes to go through individual questions which were poorly done. As with handing back any work, read out some of the more imaginative and creative correct answers, since this inspires other pupils and shows that you are taking their work seriously. Also, agree as a department what to do if pupils miss an examination or get a dreadful or erratic mark perhaps by building a minimum threshold into the tests or by some kind of review procedure.

Setting Examination Papers

The Format

1. **Consider the time allocation** for the examination. Set appropriate questions which will keep the class working for the whole of the examination, but take care not to include questions which are going to take a disproportionate amount of time. For example, setting one essay question as part of the examination is good but setting five small essays is probably inappropriate.

2. **Give guidance on the examination paper**. For example, give advice on whether to answer in a sentence, a paragraph or in an essay format. If pupils are to choose from a selection of questions make this very clear.

3. **Build in an element of differentiation** if the same examination covers a range of abilities. Ensure that shorter questions are at the beginning so that all pupils can feel they are achieving. Also make sure that you include some extension work for the more able.

4. **Always print examination papers** in order to ensure clarity.

The Tasks

1. When using **skill-based questions** identify which skill is being tested. Educate pupils in the art of tackling them.

2. Use **structured questions** which enable pupils to explore a topic in some depth and at different levels.

The Assessment

1. **Include an indication of the marks to be awarded** for each question. This should give pupils a clear idea as to how much detail should be included in their answers.

2. **Prepare a draft mark scheme** before you ask pupils to sit the examination. This will give you a guide as to the appropriateness of your questions and to the mark distribution. This draft may have to be amended in the light of some of the answers pupils give, since you cannot always account for every possible response to your question. Furthermore, you may find that your questions can be interpreted correctly in more than one way. Pupils need to be given credit for answering your question and not your interpretation of your question!

3. If possible **moderate a sample of the papers** with the department to ensure that all of your marking is of the same standard.

External Examinations

RE teachers are only too aware that operating public examination groups is far from easy. Once you have them established, the immediate challenge is maintaining pupil numbers so that groups are viable. Good examination results have always been an important part of this and, with the advent of school performance tables, examination results are placed under greater scrutiny. There are good reasons for introducing public examination syllabuses. They give the department added status in the school, they present a stimulating challenge for teachers and offer the opportunity for pupils to explore the subject at a more sophisticated level.

Establishing RE at GCSE level

Those RE teachers who move to a school where GCSE courses have not run before or have long since died out, know that the first challenge is to get RE into the options system in addition to the compulsory requirement. Present curriculum planners with the argument that pupils should have the choice of further study and that offering an examination subject will give RE parity with other humanities subjects. Argue that the first time an option group for GCSE is created, numbers may well be small and that because parents and pupils may be reluctant to give it a go, curriculum planners need to encourage 'small beginnings'. Try and get some sort of agreement in advance as to what is a viable group number. Do some research into a range of GCSE subjects to ensure RE is being treated on equal terms with other curriculum areas. Once in the system, keep a close watch on publicity and information about option choices. Sometimes, subjects get 'moved' from one column to another without a head of department being consulted and with disastrous consequences.

Schools may offer the department the choice of teaching a GCSE course during lunch-time or after school. While not ideal, this situation can be tolerated under certain circumstances: namely, that other subjects are treated in a similar fashion, that the teacher receives non-teaching time 'in lieu', that the pupils live locally and are attracted by the idea of an additional GCSE subject, and that the class does not clash with popular extra-curricular activities. The disadvantages are that teachers and pupils can be tired with an 'extra' lesson at the end of the day, that RE can be seen as an oddity and not all pupils will be attracted to these lessons.

GCSE Examinations

Currently there are five examination boards who offer both a long GCSE course in Religious Studies and a short GCSE course in Religious Education. Apart from the syllabuses, the boards usually provide specimen papers, coursework information and reports on previous year's examinations. Never assume that all boards have the same practice and check out precisely the requirements of each board. Read all the small print very carefully! It is not unusual for a syllabus to be modified, so make sure you read the relevant syllabus and associated requirements for the year in which your candidates will actually sit the examination. The addresses of the boards are given in the *Resource Guide*.

If you are setting up a GCSE course for the first time or contemplating a change from one examination board to another, send off for syllabuses from every board. You need to do this well in advance. It takes considerable time to read and assimilate the information. It is also important to start planning and preparing early. You need to be clear about your syllabus and options in good time 'to sell' to year 9 groups.

Note that sometimes schools favour one or two examination boards to save costs and administration. Check this out with your school examinations officer in advance. Finally, in choosing a specific board and syllabus consider the following:-

1. **Contact and Support:** Ideally, there should be a subject officer to give advice specifically on RE/RS. The kind of support offered should influence your decision as to which board you choose.
2. **Resources:** Analyse where your existing resources will match new requirements. If new purchases are necessary, estimate the cost. It is worth noting that some examination boards have commissioned their own text books.
3. **Staffing:** Make sure that the department are competent to teach this course and are not reliant on one person.
4. **Training:** Establish whether training will be required.

As a final point, it is generally unwise to offer pupils a choice as to which sections or options they would like to follow within a syllabus. The department should make the decision since you know what resources are available and the expertise required by teaching staff. In cases where it proves hard to make a choice, it can be helpful to seek information from others who have experience of a particular course such as other teachers, advisers or consultants.

Attracting pupils

Dynamic marketing skills are essential. Year 9 classes are your target, so aim to design an exciting year 9 syllabus which will attract pupils to the possibility of a GCSE course. Make sure you have effective classroom displays illustrating what goes on at GCSE. Useful resources available from the Christian Education Movement (CEM) include a leaflet, *Religious Education and Religious Studies: GCSE's and Beyond. What's in it for you?* and a video, *The Science of Religion*, which is geared to potential GCSE pupils.

If you are launching a course for the first time, then it may be possible to give a talk to the whole year group in assembly. Focus your eyes on form tutors as well as pupils for they will be giving advice about options. Finally, make sure you have written all the required information in option booklets, stressing the value of studying RE and the fact that no religious commitment is required. Be ready, too, with convincing arguments for parents in case they approach you.

New courses at key stage 4

Some local authorities have adapted, or are in the process of so doing, their Agreed Syllabuses to enable schools to teach either a full (RS) or short (RE) GCSE course to all pupils as their core experience. If this is your situation and the school is planning to take up a short or full course, it is important to consider time, staffing and resources. A full GCSE course in Religious Studies should have a similar time provision as a similar course in other subjects. History or geography provide good comparisons. A short course requires about 5% of curriculum time or approximately one hour per week throughout the key stage. Also, RE specialists are needed to teach examination classes and, if non-specialists are used, training will be a big issue. And, finally, some of the GCSE short courses are 'breaking new ground' with topics that are not covered in the full courses, so check that the necessary resources and funding are available.

AS and A Level Religious Studies

At the time of writing, there is a major review of post-16 education underway which will affect the teaching of all AS and A Level subjects including religious studies. In practice, it means that candidates will not be able to take an A Level without first completing an AS Level and AS Level will become the first stage of the A Level course. Candidates can then take the AS paper at the end of year 12 and the A Level (A2) paper at the end of year 13 or take both papers together at the end of year 13. The weighting of the two papers is AS, 40% and A2, 60%.

Currently, a number of schools teach years 12 and 13 together but, under the new arrangements, this may be impossible. However, AS and A pupils can be taught together as they will have common teaching material. The new syllabuses are to be examined for the first time in 1999 (AS) and 2000 (A2). Details of the examining boards are contained in the *Resource Guide*.

When setting up a new course, be prepared to argue your case with curriculum planners. Other colleagues may also need persuading, since the addition of A Level Religious Studies to an option system may mean smaller numbers for their subjects. Once you have been promised that the subject will appear, ask to be kept informed of developments. Ideally, find out the names of interested pupils and exert a little friendly pressure. Take action if you sense that they are being counselled away from Religious Studies because it is a new option. Check out beforehand what is considered to be a viable group number. Remember that two teachers are probably needed to teach an A Level course in order that the workload can be shared. A GCSE qualification is not essential for prospective AS and A Level candidates but it helps. However, there are a number of schools that do not offer a GCSE course but do offer Religious Studies at AS or A Level quite successfully. As with the establishment of a GCSE course, bear in mind the expertise of the teachers involved, avoid offering pupils a choice, decide whether there will be a need for staff training and explore the resource implications. Setting up resources for an A Level examination is costly, even if the group is small. Make sure you do some preliminary calculations and allocate your budget accordingly.

Note that the school may require certain GCSE grades in order to be accepted on A Level courses. If this is not the case in your school, consider carefully whether all interested pupils are actually suitable. In a rush of enthusiasm to build up numbers, do not be tempted to accept anyone into the group. It is especially important that candidates have good literary skills for writing essays and for arguing a viewpoint.

Then, plan your strategy for 'selling' the new examination to potential customers. Booklets, talks in assembly and at post-16 Option Evenings and even taster sessions are important. Finally, remember that preparing and delivering AS and A Level syllabuses is extremely hard work. Never underestimate the time it will take to read around the syllabus let alone plan the lessons. It is best to start preparing in the spring term of the calendar year in which you want to start the course.

Key Skills

The key skills of communication, application of number and use of IT have to be written into A Level syllabuses as appropriate. AS and A Level religious studies courses will contain the skill of communication. The criteria for all A Level subjects should contain spiritual and moral issues and be designed to promote critical thinking. Obviously, religious studies will incorporate these areas.

Keeping in touch with an examination board and its requirements

1. Make regular checks to ensure that you have all the literature produced by the board.

2. Keep all examination board information readily accessible so store it in a box file. Note the telephone number of the board and any contact person.

3. If the examination board runs any training courses for teachers, try to attend them. You could pick up valuable information and advice.

4. Obtain reading lists and past examination papers from boards which are offering similar options to the ones you have chosen. It would be confusing to show pupils materials from a board which they are not studying but it could prove beneficial to the teacher to see the different ways a question on a particular topic may be worded.

5. If possible, find out which other schools in your locality are studying for the same examination and share the experience. Sometimes examination boards may release this information. If not your local adviser may know and if all else fails, it may be worth making a few telephone calls to other schools.

Improving the Quality of Teaching and Learning

Teachers should study the chosen syllabus, options and assessment criteria very carefully. Familiarity breeds confidence and this will hopefully be communicated to pupils. All pupils should be given a copy of the relevant sections of the syllabus. Consider too, how much other information should be given to them. For example, they will definitely need to know about mark allocations for coursework and written papers.

It may be worth writing a 'guide to the examination course' for pupils and parents, listing information mentioned above plus the dates for coursework assignments. For teaching purposes the syllabus options should be divided up into manageable topics. Lessons should be extremely well prepared and detailed, with all background reading and research carried out prior to the lesson. In other words, the teacher must be thoroughly immersed in the topic before teaching it.

It is useful to establish a pattern of learning within the group. For example, operate a system of (i) a series of lessons and homework on a topic, (ii) a factual test on the topic and (iii) a timed essay (completed in class) on the topic. Never assume that pupils will automatically remember all the facts and information you give them or they research themselves. Regular testing is good preparation for examinations. For each topic, accumulate 'a bank' of questions from past examination papers.

When marking pupils' work, use the required criteria so that pupils are aware of their level of attainment. Give regular feedback to individuals, with clear evaluative comments suggesting further tasks and targets. And, as pupils complete a range of assignments, tests and coursework, make it clear to them the kind of grades you are predicting. Indicate what steps will need to be taken to improve or move up a grade. This may be particularly crucial for candidates whose future depends upon the achieving of certain grades for higher education. Encourage individual pupils to track their own performance.

Aim to get to know your examination pupils particularly well. Establish a regular homework pattern and check that pupils are delivering what is required. State assignment/coursework deadlines at the start of each term or half-term. Those who may be struggling should be helped early on. If some A Level candidates are a grave cause for concern, then talk to their form tutors and check out how they are progressing in other subjects. Don't let them continue without taking action, otherwise it becomes increasingly difficult to ask them to give up the course.

A good way of gauging the standard of examination work is for teachers to get together and moderate coursework or essays. A small RE department is advised to link up with another RE department. A match of examination board and options would be ideal but, if this cannot be achieved, teachers could show samples of examination assignments to each other. This can be a most useful exercise and helps the department become more secure in recognising the various grade boundaries.

Supporting examination pupils

- State exactly what needs to be brought to lessons and never assume that the older the pupils are, the less help they need.

- Advise pupils about the organisation of their notes. Help them improve on their note-taking skills.

- Assist pupils with essay writing skills. Talk about planning, introduction, development and conclusion in essays and arguments. Demonstrate by taking a topic from the syllabus.

- Remind them of the importance of answering the set question. Present them with model answers. If it is a small group, photocopy essays from past years to illustrate grade boundaries.

- Encourage pupils to debate, discuss and give presentations.

- As examinations approach, devise appropriate revision timetables. A revision programme needs to cover all topics either in class or for homework, or both. Buy any relevant revision guides.

There may be a need to provide additional support material in a simplified form. For example, at GCSE level comments or explanations of set biblical texts relating to moral issues can be very helpful. Sometimes, books specified on an A Level reading list can be far too complex for some pupils. However, have extension materials available for the more able pupils, so that they can further extend their knowledge and understanding and aim for top grades.

Check out what kind of source materials are available in the school or the local library, local bookshops and religious organisations or communities. Encourage pupils to read newspapers and relevant magazines and to bring into school appropriate stories, news items and editorials relating to sections of the syllabus. Make effective use of human resources in your area including students and lecturers at theological colleges, colleges of higher education and local faith communities. Ask on the RE grapevine for suitable people. Also, subscribe to any magazines specifically for AS and A Level and encourage candidates to attend national or local conferences. Details of many of these can be found in *RE Today*, published by CEM (see the *Resource Guide* for details).

As examinations approach, instruct pupils in revision techniques such as the highlighting of key points, bullet points and numbered points. Discuss flow charts, vocabulary lists and mnemonics as aids to memory and recall. Enable pupils to get into 'the language of exams' by looking at and analysing questions. Arrange extra voluntary coaching sessions at lunch-time or after school. This will really benefit pupils who are 'borderline grades' and is particularly important where you have large groups and a wide range of ability.

At A Level, if you have been teaching years 12 and 13 together, extra sessions focusing on examination technique and revision will be additionally helpful. These extra sessions should be seen as important and enjoyable. Arrange refreshments and maximise the time. A letter to parents in advance of the start of the revision programme may ensure an even better attendance. Make sure you allow opportunities for pupils to share their concerns about the examinations, either individually or corporately.

Preparing for the Examination: Notes for pupils 1 - During the Course

Revision should be something which you do throughout the course. It should not be left to the end of the course when you only have two or three weeks to cram everything in. Revision for the final public examinations should be started three or four months before the examinations begin.

After each major topic write your own summary revision notes. Some people find it helpful to use file cards. Others just list the main points learnt on a piece of file paper. Use sub-headings and bullet points. If there is anything you do not understand make sure you check it with your teacher straight away. Then:

Design a revision programme taking advantage of school holidays. Make sure that you build short breaks and treats into this timetable. This will give you something to look forward to and will help concentrate your mind for the time you are revising. The treat can be anything from a piece of cake, a phone call to a friend or listening to a favourite tape.

Preparing for the Examination:
Notes for pupils 2 - The Final Countdown

Try to revise in a warm quiet place. Most people need silence when they revise so do not try to revise whilst the television is on. Seek quietness. Libraries can sometimes be good places for concentrated periods of silence.

Try various techniques of memorising material:-
* Learn key words which stimulate thoughts.
* Repeat the same material over and over again by reading, writing and speaking aloud.
* Devise your own flow charts.
* Explain to a parent or friend what you are learning.
* Get someone to test you orally.
After you have revised a topic try an old examination question or test.

On the day of the examination:
* eat a good breakfast - brains need nourishment to work at their best;
* dress comfortably - do not wear too tight fitting clothes because examination rooms can be hot and stuffy;
* make sure that you have all the materials for the examination - check these before you leave your house. Take extra pens or pencils in case one runs out or breaks. Put all your materials in a clear plastic see through bag.

When you receive the examination paper:
* read the instructions carefully - many pupils fail examinations because they fail to follow all the instructions (sometimes they answer too many questions, wasting valuable time);
* listen carefully to the instructions of the invigilator - occasionally there is a printing error and corrections need to be made orally;
* spend the first five minutes reading through all the questions - and deciding which questions to answer.

Before answering a question:
* underline the key words and parts of the question;
* take note of how many marks are being awarded - this will give you an indication of how much detail you need to include in your answer;
* answer all the questions you have to - for example, it is better to attempt two essay questions incompletely than to answer one fully and the other not at all;
* check the time now and then to make sure that you are on course to complete the examination.

Try to leave ten minutes at the end of the examination to read through all your answers, correcting mistakes and adding details.

Analysing Examination Results

One of the first tasks of the autumn term is to analyse external examination results. Obviously GCSE, AS and A Level will need to be analysed separately. Although the task falls to the head of department, it is useful to involve other members of the department in this review as appropriate and a report should be a key agenda item for the first departmental meeting of the term. The chart overleaf sets out the main questions to ask.

Examination results: Questions to ask and action to take

Immediately:

1. Look at how many pupils achieved each grade and what percentage of the total number of pupils were awarded each grade.
2. Make a comparison with previous years. Are results improving?
3. How far did pupils achieve their predicted grades? If there are discrepancies, compare how individual pupils performed in RE or RS against their other subjects.
4. Analyse results by gender so that any underachievement can be seen and acted upon.

Later:

1. Compare your results (e.g. A-C, A-G, A-E, etc.) with other RE departments in the locality. Local authority schools should have access to the relevant data.
2. Compare your results against national averages. SCAA publishes an annual summary of examination results with national averages.
3. Compare your results with those of schools using the same and different boards.

Reflect on:

1. Whether the choice of certain options within the syllabus creates particular difficulties for pupils?
2. How representative of the full ability range were pupils in the examination groups?
3. If two or more groups of similar ability - or even a whole year group - have taken the same examination, compare results group by group. If different teachers were involved in the teaching, explore whether there are significant differences in grade outcomes.
4. Read the moderators' comments on your coursework and act on them. Read the Chief Examiner's Annual Report and note key points. Incorporate these into your future planning perhaps through targets in your development plan.
5. If you are new to examination analysis, seek help from more experienced colleagues in your own or other schools or from your adviser.

Section 9.
MONITORING RE

This section is designed to support teachers running an RE department with responsibility for one or more other teachers who may be specialists or non-specialists.

Internal Monitoring

Internal monitoring simply means to check, observe and note what is happening in religious education in your school. This will not be difficult if there is only one person, namely yourself, involved in the department. However, even if there is only one other person for whom you are responsible, it is essential that you have a clear strategy in place. Should you be in a position where you have a large number of teachers involved in the delivery of RE, monitoring then becomes a key task for you on a regular basis. It is important to remember that monitoring can uncover good as well as bad practice. You must also expect that action will follow on from your findings. Through monitoring you are seeking to raise standards and improve the quality of teaching and learning.

Providing a context for monitoring

From the outset, make it clear through departmental meetings, or individual conversations if not all teachers can attend meetings, that you will operate a system of monitoring. Be sure to explain the purpose and practicalities involved in this. That should then reduce any anxiety when you inform a colleague that you will be visiting his or her classroom.

Make sure that you have copies of timetables for all those teaching RE. It may be that you can get a print-out of this. Display this information in a prominent position in your office or classroom, so that you can see at a glance which year groups are being taught RE in which rooms, by whom and at what time. Careful analysis of everyone's timetables, including your own, will indicate your availability for watching colleagues' lessons. If it transpires that you are never 'free' to watch certain year groups or teachers, then you will want to discuss this situation with a member of the senior management team or the school's professional tutor. It may be that some cover can be provided for your lessons while you carry out the monitoring.

Aim for a consistent approach in the implementation of policies. This means that everyone teaching RE must be clear about what is expected of them. For example, at the start of the school year, a reminder of departmental policies should be given to all those teaching RE. This might involve a focus on new initiatives in particular areas.

Although no two RE teachers have identical styles and approaches, encourage a consistent approach towards lesson planning. You may want to design a standard form for lesson planning or there may be a general one used across all departments. The rationale for a standard form is that the teachers using it are likely to give thought to the same areas in planning. This should then result in a more thorough and consistent delivery across a year group.

Monitoring lessons

Once you have decided which teachers and classes you are able to observe, do inform the member of staff in advance of the lesson. It is not unusual for some teachers, and particularly non-specialists, to feel a little nervous when observed, so aim to have a conversation about the lesson before the observation time. Request a lesson plan and state what role you, as the observer, will take. For example, will you just sit at the back and make notes, or will you involve yourself in the lesson?

Either observe a full lesson or negotiate aspects to observe. It is advisable to spend part of the lesson sitting at the back observing the teaching and learning process. It is also helpful if the format of the lesson allows for you to talk to pupils about what they are doing and have a look through their exercise books.

Notes should be made about the lesson. You could use, or design, an appropriate form. Many heads of department favour the OFSTED lesson observation form used during school inspections. The following page gives a different example showing some of the questions to pose. Alternatively, you may like to simply make notes using some prompts. Whatever notes you make, include any strengths and weaknesses of the teaching and comment on how pupils respond to the lesson.

Even if you have to rush off at the end of the lesson in order to teach another class, do make a brief comment to the teacher. Space must then be made for debriefing and discussion, preferably on the same day. You may like to begin by asking the teacher how he or she thought the lesson had gone. Make sure you clearly state strengths of the lesson before elaborating on any weaknesses. Set any appropriate targets for improvement and end on a positive note. If you are only observing certain aspects do not comment on other things you notice, unless asked to.

Monitoring written work

Another useful method of gauging how RE is being delivered and what progress pupils are making, is to sample a range of exercise books or files. It is hoped that all pupils in a particular year group will have a similar RE experience. To check this out, scrutinise work across a year group and monitor content, presentation and teacher assessment. This is not to suggest that individual teachers are to be given no freedom in their approach or delivery. What needs to be checked is that the same areas of content are being covered and that work is marked regularly and according to departmental guidelines. Whatever the outcome of this exercise, it must be shared with departmental colleagues. If a number of teachers are not doing as required then this would make a key agenda item for the next departmental meeting. If it is just one teacher who is not following agreed practice, a private conversation is clearly essential.

Of course, it is perfectly possible for all members of the RE department to monitor work in exercise books as part of a meeting, in which case you could call the agenda item 'Moderation'. This can be a very productive activity as teachers look at pupil progress across a year group and learn from one another. If you have a newly qualified or recently trained teacher in your department, the school's professional tutor or other senior staff may observe these teachers in RE lessons. If this is the case, make sure you get some feedback as to how the RE lessons are going.

LESSON OBSERVATION

ASPECTS	QUESTIONS TO ASK	✓ or comment
PLANNING	• is planning adequate and appropriate? • how does the lesson fit into overall RE programme? • if relevant - how does the lesson relate to a syllabus?	
START OF LESSON	• are teacher and pupils punctual? • is there a prompt start to the lesson? • are aims and objectives shared with pupils?	
TEACHING	• does the lesson follow the prepared plan? • does the teacher motivate pupils and sustain their interest? • is an attempt made to involve all pupils in the lesson? • is there effective communication of religious ideas and concepts? • does the teacher have a sound grasp of the material being taught? • are pupils praised and encouraged? • are contributions affirmed as appropriate? • are the tasks, activities and resources relevant for the pupils and the aspect of religion being taught? • is the RE content related to pupils' interests and experiences where possible? • are opportunities provided for pupils to reflect and respond? • is discussion 'handled' in an atmosphere of mutual respect? • is the teacher enthusiastic about RE? • does the room display support learning? • are pupils building on prior learning? • have pupils understood what is required of them?	
LEARNING	• how do pupils of different ability levels respond to the lesson? • does teacher input and activities enable pupils to make progress during the lesson? • is there understanding of religious ideas or concepts? • are pupils able to relate material to their daily lives? • are pupils developing skills in the use of religious language? • is there evidence (discussion or writing) that pupils are exploring, reflecting on and evaluating their own views and those of others?	

ASPECTS	QUESTIONS TO ASK	✔ or comment
LEARNING	• do pupils know about and understand the range of religious traditions represented in Great Britain? Can they name them? • are pupils able to talk about the religion/aspect they are currently studying? • do pupils display positive attitudes towards RE? • do pupils pose searching questions? • what can pupils do as a result of this lesson?	
GENERAL	• are teacher-pupil relationships supportive of learning? • are there examples of poor behaviour or inappropriate contributions and how does the teacher respond? • what is the general atmosphere of lesson? • are support staff present and how does the teacher relate to them? • is pupils' written work regularly marked according to requirements?	
CLOSE OF LESSON	• did the lesson follow the plan? Were any deviations appropriate? • did teacher suitably summarise the material covered and make links to past and future lessons? • was homework required or set? • how did the group leave?	

External Inspection

This section of the unit considers the formal inspection of RE by outside agencies. At intervals of six years or less, all maintained schools are inspected by OFSTED and as part of the process the RE department will be inspected. In Church-Aided schools, RE will receive a special denominational inspection from someone specially trained for this task. In addition to OFSTED inspecting some private schools, the independent sector has its own arrangements for inspection and, once again, RE will generally feature in the process.

The advice that follows provides guidance on how to plan for, survive, and possibly even benefit from an RE inspection. Although much of the information given will apply to the OFSTED system of inspection, it should be of help to any RE teacher preparing for inspection under other regulations. However, it is vital to obtain the relevant literature and information from the respective inspection agency concerned with your type of school whether it be OFSTED, Diocesan Guidelines for Church Schools or the Independent Schools Inspection Service.

The following page shows a simplified version of the kind of inspection form used for OFSTED lesson observation.

The 'OFSTED' lesson observation form

Context of the Observation

Grade 0-7   Evidence and Evaluation

Teaching   ☐

Response   ☐

Attainment   ☐

Progress   ☐

Other significant evidence

Use grades 0 or 1-7 with: 0 = insufficient evidence 2 = very good / well above average
4 = satisfactory / about average 6 = poor / well below average

Preparing for inspection The key message is to be prepared. There is no doubt that the inspection process can cause anxiety for some teachers but the most effective way of alleviating some of the possible stress is to ensure you are ready for the process well in advance. These are the main areas to cover before an inspection:

1. **Documentation:** Most RE teachers will already have documentation in the form of an RE handbook. You do not have to provide information relating to the areas that covers but it is helpful for the visiting inspector to have access to written details about the department before, and during, the week of inspection.

2. **Monitoring:** If a number of teachers are involved in the teaching of RE it will be useful for the head of department to spend some time monitoring.

3. **Pre-Inspection Support:** It may be possible to ask your local authority, diocese, or adviser to carry out a day of pre-inspection support - visiting lessons, looking at documentation and feeding back recommendations. There are also independent consultants who specialise in this area and can provide excellent feedback.

4. **Department Meetings:** Spend time discussing the inspection process so everyone in the department is familiar with the process. A specialist handbook will help you with this.

The inspection process The time an RE inspector will spend in a school will vary but the main purpose of an RE inspection is to check that statutory and school requirements are being met and to assess the quality and standards of RE. In addition, a whole range of related factors will be considered. However, not all these factors will be mentioned in the final written report by the RE inspector.

How do inspectors collect evidence?

Through:

- observation of lessons;
- talking to RE teachers;
- reading departmental documentation including schemes of work, the department handbook and teacher planning documents;
- talking to pupils;
- looking at pupils' work.

It is important to realise that it is a combination of the above activities that will contribute to the findings about RE in a particular school. Also, note that it is the observation of many lessons and possibly several teachers that all have to be taken into account as judgements are finally made. Clearly, lesson observations are key in the whole process because they reveal details about pupil attainment and progress, attitudes to learning and the skills shown by teachers. However, other related factors play a part, such as the management of the department, resources and accommodation.

The framework and guidance documents that inspectors refer to cover a range of headings and, for each one, a series of questions is listed. The questions posed below are typical of the kind that inspectors may be trying to answer as they carry out their work. It is important to note that, although many questions are posed here under a single heading, the inspector will not expect to find evidence for all of those areas within one lesson.

1. Teaching

Subject Expertise
- Are teachers qualified in RE? Has each teacher the necessary knowledge and understanding to teach the designated course?
- Is the teacher familiar with the course requirements and associated syllabus?
- Does he or she have the ability to successfully communicate religious ideas and concepts and relate these to pupils' interests and experiences?
- Does he or she have the ability and knowledge to sustain discussion and debate on religious and moral issues?

Subject Planning
- Are lessons or units of work planned adequately? Who is responsible for planning?
- Are lessons based on the relevant syllabus requirements?
- Are there clear specific objectives for each lesson with detail as to how these will be achieved?
- Do tasks and activities match the needs of all pupils? What is the composition of the teaching group?

Challenge and Expectations
- Are all pupils challenged to achieve high standards in written and discussion work?
- Are pupils encouraged to understand and debate complex religious ideas, concepts and controversies?
- Are pupils encouraged to relate religious and moral issues to daily living?
- Are activities and tasks engaging and motivating all pupils?
- Are teachers aware of pupils' strengths and weaknesses so that pupils can make appropriate progress?
- Is homework an integral part of the RE curriculum? Is it checked and marked regularly?

Teaching Methods and Classroom Organisation
- Are a wide range of teaching methods used, e.g. direct teaching about world faiths, individual research, group work, class discussion, learning from videos and visitors?
- Are religions presented as 'living faiths'?
- Are pupils encouraged to consider, respect and value people whatever faith or belief stance they may hold?
- Are opportunities created for the discussion of religious issues in an atmosphere of mutual respect?
- Do methods and skills of organisation promote high standards in RE?

Use of Time and Resources
- Is there a good pace to the lesson enabling objectives to be met and pupils to be kept on task?
- Are resources appropriate, so that pupils are getting the most out of them?
- How do teachers support pupils throughout the lesson? How do they respond to pupils, encourage or praise them and deal with inappropriate or inaccurate answers?
- Is time spent at the close of the lesson for pupils to reflect on what has been achieved?

2. Pupil Attainment and Progress

- In different age groups and at key stages, how do pupils' attainments in RE compare with national standards and expectations? Consider pupils of high, medium and low ability and those with special needs.
- How do past and current GCSE and A Level results compare with national standards?
- Is there any significant variation in attainment among pupils of different gender, ethnicity or background?
- In each year group or key stage, what knowledge, understanding and skills do pupils have in relation to the religions they are studying? Are they familiar with religious concepts and can they use appropriate terminology? What are their strengths and weaknesses?
- Given the current levels of attainment pupils have achieved and are achieving, has significant progress been made? Consider with reference to high, average, low attaining and special needs pupils. Is there any evidence of underachievement?

3. Pupil Response, Attitude and Behaviour

- How are pupils responding to RE? Is there a sense of enjoyment and interest in the lessons? Can pupils explain the value of religious education?
- What is the take-up for GCSE and A Level courses in RE and RS?
- During lessons is there sustained concentration, co-operation between pupils and teacher and collaboration (when required) between pupils?
- Do pupils display enquiry skills, perseverance, confidence? Do they ask searching questions?
- Are pupils formulating their views on religious issues and developing maturity of thought?
- Are pupils analysing and evaluating their own and other people's beliefs and values?

4. The RE Curriculum

- What are the legal requirements for RE in this kind of school? Are they fulfilled? Consider what requirements are stipulated or recommended in syllabuses or elsewhere.
- Does the timetable's provision for RE enable the relevant syllabus to be taught? Many syllabuses recommend 5% of curriculum time. What is the RE provision in each year group?
- How have decisions been made about which religions to teach?

- Is the RE curriculum providing breadth and balance over each term and year? Consider the number of religions taught and the approach taken.
- Are there schemes of work for each year group? Overall, is continuity and progression evident between and across year groups?
- Is curriculum planning weak, adequate or strong?
- Does the teaching of RE take place during the official school day or is there any extra-curricular provision? Consider whether GCSE lessons are taught during the lunch-break or after school.
- Do any pupils withdraw from RE lessons? What happens to them during this time?
- What examination courses are offered? Consider GCSE Religious Studies (Full), GCSE Religious Education (Short), AS and A Level Religious Studies.
- How are classes organised for RE? Are they mixed-ability, banded or in sets?

5. Assessing, Recording, Reporting

- Is there a policy for Assessment, Recording and Reporting (ARR)? If so does it meet the requirements of the school and its syllabus?
- Do all the RE staff implement the policy consistently, or has it not been agreed?
- Are a range of tasks used for assessment purposes?
- To what extent does assessment provide feedback to pupils, inform teacher planning and support continuity and progression?
- Are pupils ever involved in assessing and recording their own work? Does the school offer a record of achievement?
- How does the RE department record pupil progress including SEN pupils? Is there a departmental portfolio of work?
- Is there an annual report on individual progress in RE as required in maintained schools? Do reports actually comment on progress? Against what is this measured?

6. Equal Opportunities

- Is there equality of access to the RE curriculum for all pupils? Consider any withdrawals for additional language support or examination options.
- Is the RE teaching sensitive to the different viewpoints, cultures and religions represented in the school and the wider community?
- Are teaching materials and displays produced with due regard to gender, cultural and religious balance?

7. Leadership, Management and Co-ordination of the RE Department

- Does the head of department have a clear job description? Is it carried out? Is there vision and purpose in the department?
- Are members of the RE department suitably led, supported and professionally developed? Consider especially any non-specialists.
- Are there regular departmental meetings and are they suitably documented?
- What is the quality of relationships within the RE department?
- Is there a 'shared ethos' within the team? Who is involved in decision making?

- Do departmental policies and practices reflect overall school aims and objectives and those listed in the school development plan?
- Is there adequate planning and a structured evaluation and review of departmental practice? Is there an RE development plan with appropriate targets set?
- Is there effective monitoring of the RE teaching across all year groups to ensure consistency of delivery?
- Is there an effective RE profile around the school? How is RE communicated to other groups such as parents and governors?
- Does the quality of leadership and co-ordination contribute to the standards achieved in RE?

8. Spiritual, Moral, Social and Cultural Development (SMSC)

- How far does the RE department promote and provide opportunities for SMSC development? Consider schemes of work.
- Is there a departmental policy on SMSC development?

9. Special Educational Needs (SEN)

- How are the needs of SEN pupils met through the RE curriculum? Consider make-up of teaching groups, teaching and learning strategies and the RE curriculum itself.
- How are RE teachers made aware of pupils with SEN? Are there procedures in place?
- What is the link between the Special Needs Department Co-ordinator and RE teachers?
- How is any in-class support agreed and do support staff work effectively in RE lessons?
- What kinds of material resources are available to support pupils across the range of ability levels?

10. Staffing

- How many specialists and non-specialists teach RE? What percentage of lessons are taught by non-specialists? Is there any correlation between the non-specialists and the quality of teaching, learning and standards achieved?
- Does the number of specialist RE teachers 'match' the requirements of the RE curriculum enabling it to be taught effectively to all pupils?
- What INSET and professional development opportunities have staff been involved in both internally and externally?
- What is the status of the person in charge of RE? Consider title, allocation of responsibilities and remuneration in terms of time and money.
- What is the role of support staff in RE lessons?

11. Learning Resources

- Is there a good range of all types of resources so that the RE curriculum can be taught well? Does the range meet the needs of pupils of varying abilities on different courses?
- Are resources sufficient in quantity so that all year groups have access to relevant materials? Consider the quantity of text books available if two classes of the same year group are being taught at the same time, and the use of text books for homework.
- What is the quality of the RE resources? Are there stimulating accessible texts that present gender and cultural diversity in a positive way?
- Does the RE department have a class library? What use is made of the school library? Are pupils aware of relevant materials?
- Does the RE department make use of any loan services through the local education authority or RE Centres?
- What use is made of visits and visitors?
- Do pupils have access to information technology facilities? Is there any evidence of pupils making use of information technology skills in the production of their work?
- What is the annual funding of the RE department? How does the department evaluate its spending? Is the deployment of resources effective and efficient?

12. Accommodation

- Is there a designated RE teaching room with adequate storage facilities?
- Is there adequate space within teaching room(s) for group work and the movement of tables?
- How far does the accommodation promote or inhibit teaching and learning in RE? Consider equipment including television, videotape recorder, overhead projector, furniture, fabric, and general decor.
- Are there effective RE displays with a balance between pupils' work and commercially produced materials?

Section 10. MANAGING THE DEPARTMENT

This section of the book should help teachers who are already in post as, or aspire to become, the head of an RE department or who are taking on new management responsibilities.

The Role of the Head of Department

Schools are different and people are different. There is no 'right' way to run a department. However, there are plans, and strategies which have to be addressed. In schools, heads of department are sometimes called 'middle managers' but there are also other types of manager. Look around your school and reflect on how different managers, the headteacher, deputy heads and heads of year for example, operate in their particular roles. It is clear that people work in different ways and often change or adapt their style as they are involved in a range of situations.

Therefore, the first thing to do as head of department is to reflect on your own style of management. Once you are aware of it, then you will be in a better position to adapt your approach as different needs arise. In time, this should turn you into a more effective manager.

Look at your job description. It may be a generic document or it may be subject specific. Generally, all tasks listed on a job description will fall into one of two categories: managing people and managing tasks. An effective head of department will demonstrate that he or she can manage both people and tasks effectively. This is your challenge.

Typical tasks for the head of RE

Managing People involves:
- Creating an RE identity through developing a team spirit;
- Liaising with RE team members and other staff and representing the RE team at co-ordinating meetings;
- Contacting and briefing governors, local education authority support staff;
- Encouraging departmental staff to build on their strengths;
- Enabling weaknesses to be eliminated or minimised.

Managing Tasks involves:
- Creating clear informative documentation;
- Constructing and working to an agreed development plan;
- Effectively managing and organising resources including staffing, materials and budgets;
- Keeping to regular and structured agendas at team meetings;
- Reflecting and evaluating policies in line with the department development plan.

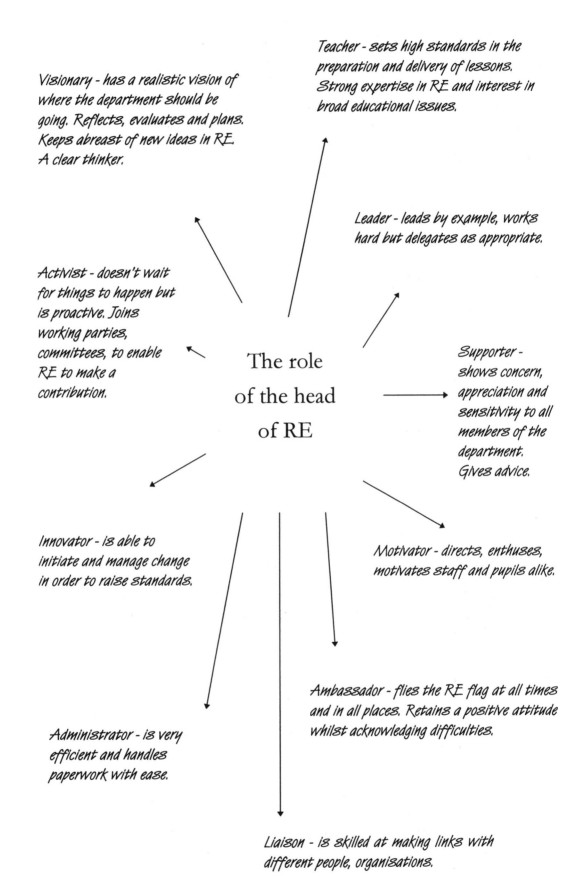

Visionary - has a realistic vision of where the department should be going. Reflects, evaluates and plans. Keeps abreast of new ideas in RE. A clear thinker.

Teacher - sets high standards in the preparation and delivery of lessons. Strong expertise in RE and interest in broad educational issues.

Activist - doesn't wait for things to happen but is proactive. Joins working parties, committees, to enable RE to make a contribution.

Leader - leads by example, works hard but delegates as appropriate.

The role of the head of RE

Supporter - shows concern, appreciation and sensitivity to all members of the department. Gives advice.

Innovator - is able to initiate and manage change in order to raise standards.

Motivator - directs, enthuses, motivates staff and pupils alike.

Ambassador - flies the RE flag at all times and in all places. Retains a positive attitude whilst acknowledging difficulties.

Administrator - is very efficient and handles paperwork with ease.

Liaison - is skilled at making links with different people, organisations.

Starting Out as a New Head of RE

Once you have been successful in obtaining a post, then you must prepare yourself for this new, challenging role. Transition to a new post is not always easy since you are completing one job and about to start another. Aim to spend at least one day in your new school before you take up the post formally. Ensure you have access to general information about the school such as staff handbooks, prospectus and pupil and staff lists. Find out as much as you can about the RE department. Look at documentation, resource lists, timetables and room allocations. Try and meet all members of the department, even those non-specialists who are only teaching the odd class or two. If possible, spend time talking to the outgoing head of RE. You may not want to inform him or her about your plans but you can often pick up useful points of information. Make an appointment with the headteacher or a deputy to check on your responsibilities, such as your tutor group, days and times of scheduled meetings and your job description.

Find out about the background and governance of the school. For example, if it is a local authority school, is there general information to which you should have access? Get to know the layout of the school and introduce yourself to some of the key people around the campus including the caretaker and office staff.

After your visit, make your own plans and priorities. You can't do everything at once but you need to establish yourself as a new head of department early on. Think how you will do this. Re-read your job description and create a departmental plan. To do this you will need to think of all aspects of the department including documentation, policies, resources, staffing, management strategies and meetings.

Managing Staffing

If you are appointed as the head of the RE department in a reasonably large school then you may well have a fully qualified RE specialist working with you. Even if this person is not highly experienced such a situation provides a wonderful opportunity to work together and create a departmental identity. There are particular ways to support an inexperienced colleague who is also a specialist. These include regular observation, checking lesson plans on a regular basis, doing joint planning for particular topics, providing opportunities for the teacher to observe your teaching, regular meetings and the maintenance of an open, communicative relationship so that the less experienced teacher feels able to share concerns and ask for help.

It is also valuable to encourage the development of responsibilities and skills which offer a breadth of experience so that your colleague has the chance to take on roles that might be considered the department head's such as checking and ordering resources, drafting internal examination papers and planning coursework. However, at the same time, beware of overloading a very inexperienced colleague.

Managing the non-specialist

It is a fact of life that in a vast number of schools there are non-specialists teaching RE. Sometimes this can cause particular difficulties and frustrations for the head of department not all of which can be easily resolved. The chart on the facing page identifies the commonest issues and suggests ways in which they can be tackled.

Issues Raised By Non-Specialists Teaching RE

The issue:

Possible resolution:

1. Often staff who can't be fitted in elsewhere or who have more free time than they should have are asked to teach RE.

   Press for staff who are known to be good teachers. Request staffing early, perhaps people you had last year. No-one can be forced to teach RE (teachers can opt out on grounds of conscience and the department does not want reluctant teachers).

2. It is sometimes said that 'anyone can teach RE'.

   It is not an easy subject. Stress the expertise and skills needed to cope with several religions and challenging questions from pupils.

3. Some think that a teacher with a particular faith or belief will be excellent in the classroom.

   Not always the case! RE is concerned with education, not instruction or indoctrination but a personal faith perspective can be a useful resource.

4. Some non-specialists may feel they cannot put enough time in to prepare, deliver and assess RE work along with other subjects they are teaching.

   This is not good enough. Each teacher has a responsibility for the pupils he or she is teaching. Department instructions and policy should be followed.

5. Sometimes non-specialists have low expectations in RE classrooms.

   This is not acceptable. RE must be treated like any other subject. Heads of RE should make this clear.

6. Non-specialists may feel inadequate because they are not 'experts' in several religions.

   Few heads of RE (if any) are experts in all the major religions. Heads of RE should provide good teaching materials but non-specialists should spend adequate time preparing for the lesson.

7. Non-specialists worry that they will be unable to answer pupils' questions and may give inaccurate information.

   It is acceptable for RE teachers to say 'I don't know'. Although it is not possible to anticipate all questions pupils may ask, again it is important for teachers to prepare thoroughly.

8. Some non-specialists may have been teaching RE for several years and a curriculum deputy suggests they can now teach GCSE.

   Examination courses especially need qualified teachers with expertise in syllabus content. Some non-specialists could perhaps manage with additional INSET but it may be time to press for another RE specialist.

If, as is often the case, your department does have several non-specialists teaching within it, you need to learn how to manage them. For example, if non-specialists cannot attend departmental meetings because they belong to several departments, they still need your support, so write notes for them or plan to see them one lunchtime. Consider an evening meal and meeting. It can create a pleasant atmosphere as well as getting business done. It is important to remember that, as the head of department, you have a responsibility to know what is going on in lessons and the work of all teachers should be monitored from time to time.

A common situation occurs when you have some highly experienced non-specialist teachers working in your department but they are so busy with other responsibilities that they are not 'pulling their weight.' You are the head of RE and you must deal with this situation. View the involvement of senior staff as a bonus. It is a superb opportunity for them to be enlightened about the department and you can demonstrate the excellent workings of your team. However, you should still expect high standards from all those teaching RE and endeavour to create a strong departmental identity. This is not always easy but it needs to be done. Give everyone plenty of help and encouragement. Hopefully, colleagues will be so impressed by the RE department, its quality of management and the interesting subject matter, that they request to teach RE again. Who knows - some of these non-specialists may turn out to be great allies for RE.

As RE expands in your school, be ready to argue the case for another specialist teacher or two. Although at the time of writing RE has been recognised as a shortage subject, this problem has been 'masked' in many schools by non-specialists teaching RE. Some non-specialists will be good value and do an excellent job but, in other situations, the quality of learning and teaching can be adversely affected.

Ten ways to develop a team ethos

1. Get to know your colleagues. This does not just mean 'talking RE' with them but getting to know them as individuals through spending time alongside them. Show interest in their lives and share their concerns.

2. Communicate on a regular basis. Keep them 'in the picture' about RE matters and ask for their ideas.

3. Be prepared for people to disagree with you but endeavour to agree on key issues like departmental procedures and policies.

4. Make clear that you are the leader and at the end of the day you are accountable and have to take final decisions. Make sure everyone understands this.

5. Treat all members of your team equally. People are different but there should be no favouritism. Do not be bribed over matters like the allocation of teaching groups!

6. Do not gossip behind people's backs.

7. Ooze confidence to your team. Try and think carefully before you act and don't panic.

8. Acknowledge difficulties within the team but always give lots of encouragement and appreciative comments.

9. If you have a large team to weld together, consider a series of team building exercises. Alternatively, consider getting the team together for a meal with an opportunity to build relationships.

10. Support the team in conversations with senior managers and other staff. Where there are problems discuss them in an open and supportive way looking for solutions.

Managing Student Teachers

At the time of writing there have been discussions concerning a new national curriculum for teacher training. Until such a curriculum becomes a legal requirement, guidance on the teaching competencies that should be developed during initial teacher training has been given by the DfEE in *Circular 9/92*. Training institutions and their partner schools need to work together to enable the student to gain a range of set competencies that include:

- an understanding of the knowledge, concepts and skills of RE (2.2.1);
- knowledge and understanding of the local Agreed Syllabus and examination syllabuses (2.2.2);
- the ability to produce coherent lesson plans (2.3.1);
- ensuring continuity and progression within and between classes and in subjects (2.3.2);
- the ability to set appropriately demanding expectations for pupils (2.3.3);
- employing a range of teaching strategies (2.2.4);
- the ability to create and maintain a purposeful and orderly environment for the pupils (2.4.2);
- demonstrating that they understand the importance of reporting to pupils on their progress and of marking their work regularly against agreed criteria (2.5.5);
- developing an understanding of the school as an institution and its place within the community (2.6.1);
- developing a working knowledge of their pastoral, contractual, legal and administrative responsibilities as teachers (2.6.2);

The head of department and a professional tutor is responsible for monitoring the development of these competencies in students. Having a student in the RE department can be beneficial but is also demanding. At its simplest, initial teacher training institutions often give the school an amount of money per student which can feed back to the department and, of course, a good student can be an enormous benefit. However, before accepting a student into the RE department you need to be confident that you can answer the following questions positively:

1. Is your department ready to work with a student? Do you, or someone within your department, have enough time to devote to the training of a student?

2. Can you offer the student a range of teaching experiences and an appropriate variety of classes throughout the age and ability range?

3. Will your department be given any funding? Who, for example, will pay for on-site costs such as photocopying?

4. Will you be given time for training the student?

5. Is it possible to find a match between your school's requirements, such as examination syllabus requirements, and the qualifications of a student?

6. Does the training institution have an RE handbook which clearly provides you with a detailed description of the training course, together with reading requirements?

Once you decide to have a student, you then have responsibilities towards him or her. Before a student starts a placement with you they will carry out a number of day visits in order to get to know your school. During these visits, work out the timetable that your student will be covering to enable him or her to prepare for the courses he or she will be teaching. Also, provide a copy of (or extracts from) your syllabus, appropriate external examination syllabuses, the key text books for use with your pupils and school policy documents. Many students find it useful to spend some time following a pupil around the school, allowing them to see a day from the pupil's point of view, as well as a range of teaching and learning styles.

Making teaching practice a success

Set clear objectives for the whole period of teaching practice. For example, by the end of the teaching practice you could reasonably expect the student to have designed a wall display using pupils' work, to have collected a portfolio of pupils' work, to have designed a booklet of worksheets and teaching notes around one of the courses which has been taught and to have helped on a field trip run by the department.

Structure lesson observation. Students will often be required to observe other teachers with their classes. It is helpful if you set clear criteria for these observation periods, covering aspects such as how to introduce and end a lesson, how to use artefacts, how to encourage class discussion or how to develop a concept. The student should collect notes on what has been observed and have the opportunity of discussing his or her findings.

Set aside time for a weekly meeting with your student. This time should be kept sacrosanct and take place in a room without distractions. It is a time in which you can set agendas and monitor progress. It is helpful at this meeting to identify specific aims for each week. To concentrate on two or three objectives can bring about quicker results than just making general observations. These objectives can be assessed at the end of each week. Also, students should attend all department meetings.

Expect students to produce clear, coherent lesson plans, and keep these neatly in a file for you to see at any time. In the early stages it will be important for you to plan the lesson alongside your student. Many students find it helpful if you show them your lesson plans - this sets clear expectations. It is also good practice to encourage them to hand you copies of their lesson plans at least a day before the lesson is to be taught. This means that you can discuss any issues which may arise out of them.

Constructive observation by the head of department enables a student to improve. Before you observe, let the student spend a few minutes talking through the lesson plan with you. This will enable you to have a clear idea of their general awareness and expectations. Once you have agreed the objectives for the week you can negotiate when to come into the lessons. For example, if you have agreed to focus in on the beginning of lessons you can come into the first ten minutes or so of quite a number of lessons. However, it is important to sit through a whole lesson at least once a week in order to obtain an overview. Give feedback as soon as possible and certainly within the same day. Once a week a student should be given detailed written feedback on at least one lesson.

Many teacher training institutions provide observation record sheets and will ask you to use these and submit them at regular intervals. If not, you can devise your own observation sheet. In the early stages of teaching practice, many students find it helpful to carry out some team teaching with the regular teacher of the class. This enables them to take charge for a small part of the lesson whilst, at the same time, learning alongside an experienced specialist. Discuss the department's and school's marking and assessment policy with the students. Before you ask students to mark work, share some of your own marking with them and in the early stages it is helpful for students to co-mark with you.

The institution of higher education is responsible for validating the quality of the student's work, awarding the qualification and recommending that they receive full teacher status. Each student will be assigned a college tutor who will co-ordinate their training and provide a link between the institution of higher education and the school. As head of department you will need to liaise with the college tutor to evaluate progress, submit written observation forms and provide reports during the period of initial teacher training. You will probably see much more of the student than the college tutor so your comments are vitally important.

Finally, in *Circular 9/92* (DfEE, 1992), there is a comment that initial teacher training should provide the necessary foundation to develop 'a readiness to promote the moral and spiritual well-being of pupils' (2.6.8.). Sometimes, RE students will ask if they can organise or lead an act of collective worship or an assembly, however, an RE student should not be expected to.

LESSON COMMENT FORM

Student Teacher   Class   Date   Time

Prepared lesson content ....

MANAGEMENT OF LESSON	WEAK	SATISFACTORY	STRONG
Student has materials, supplies and equipment ready at the start of the lesson			
Student begins the lesson quickly			
Student gets pupils on task quickly at the beginning of the lesson or activity			
Student maintains a high level of pupil time on-task			
Organisation of pupils			
Student has established a set of rules and procedures that work during the lesson			
Movement and deportment			
Speech			
Pace of lesson			
Use of writing board, overhead projector, worksheets, etc.			
Clarity of presentation			
Appropriateness of material to: class and individuals			
Safety			
RELATIONSHIPS WITH PUPILS			
Attitude towards pupils			
Attitudes of pupils			
Classroom Management: class and individuals			
Use of pupil contribution			
Class discussion			
Other comments:			

Managing Departmental Meetings

In most schools, departmental meetings are planned into the calendar on a regular basis and staff are expected to attend. What happens if you are the sole member of the RE department? Are you expected to hold a meeting with yourself? The answer is a definite 'yes' and you use the time to reflect, plan and evaluate. There will never be a shortage of tasks but it is important that you keep a record of how you have spent your time. This need not be written up in any great detail, a side of A4 will probably suffice. It may be that departmental heads are required to submit agendas and minutes of meetings so this is when your own record is invaluable. It also demonstrates effective use of time and keeps up the profile of RE in the school.

If your school has a more flexible approach to the planning of departmental meetings and it is left up to the head of department to call staff together, then make sure you establish a regular pattern. Let it be known that the RE department is organised and meets regularly.

What happens if you are running a department but the other teachers who help belong to several other departments? This is a real difficulty and you will need to sort out a system that works well for everyone. In some schools, a solution has been found by naming alternate weeks as 'Week A' and 'Week B' and giving specific departments priority in calling meetings in one or other of them. This means that if you don't get your non-specialist staff in Week A, you will certainly get them in Week B. You would obviously run a similar agenda on both occasions. If your school could usefully benefit from this system, why not suggest it? If a teacher is shared between several departments and he or she never makes the RE meeting, you may have to organise a lunch-time or after school meeting to keep him or her in touch with what's going on.

Planning the agenda

Bearing in mind your RE development plan (to which you should be working) consider the whole of the school year and the events that will be taking place during each term. Ensure that open evenings, options evening, internal examinations, external examinations, and inservice which will impact on the RE teachers' professional responsibilities, are placed on an agenda at an appropriate time. Week by week other issues will arise and you will need to decide which ones to add to your agenda. Frequently, each department may be required to discuss general school matters. This is an excellent opportunity for the RE department to contribute to a current debate or issue. Be sure to ask members of the RE department if there are matters they would like to place on the agenda.

Once you have decided on your agenda, consider whether to put a time limit for each item and ensure that colleagues receive it a few days before the meeting. It's most unhelpful for someone to find a meeting's agenda in a staff pigeon hole at 3.30 p.m. when the meeting starts at 4.00 p.m. So, be efficient and give colleagues sufficient time to reflect on the agenda so that they can make a worthwhile contribution to the meeting. Also indicate any documents or papers which need to be read and brought along.

Running the meeting

Make sure you are prepared and organised for all the items on the agenda. Gather together any notes you need and jot down points which you might forget. Try to anticipate any difficulties which may arise. Arrange the seating - several chairs around a table is probably best. Serve refreshments if you can. A plate of biscuits or even a cake usually helps create the right atmosphere. One option is to arrange festive food as appropriate such as simnel cake or potato latkas.

If possible, take notes during the meeting which will become the minutes. If you don't take notes, ensure you write up the minutes very soon, preferably the same evening. In some schools, teachers take turns at writing the minutes. Start and finish the meeting promptly. If you overrun, consider whether it would be best to postpone the discussion and continue at a later meeting. Ask others present what they think, but you take the decision. After the meeting, reflect on how you chaired. Could your style be improved? Chat to other heads of department occasionally to find out how they run their meetings.

Writing minutes of meetings - what to include

The date and time: 'Minutes of the RE Departmental Meeting held on the 3rd November 1996, 3.30 - 5.30 p.m.'

Apologies: (list any received)
Present: (list those attending)

The minutes of the previous meeting:
Matters arising:
Referrals from other committees:
Other items: (separately numbered)
Any other business: (including items for future meetings)

Closure time: ('The meeting closed at 5.30 p.m.')
Signature(s):   (the head of department and whoever wrote the minutes)

The agendas and minutes should be kept carefully in a file. Such documentation gives a helpful picture of how a department is developing and you may be asked to produce this file for a visiting inspector. Make sure that all members of the RE department receive the minutes in good time before the next meeting. If senior staff also require a copy, arrange for this to happen. Also, keep copies of any memos or letters that are written and sent as the result of a departmental meeting. Ensure they are dated.

Five ways to vary the format of a departmental meeting

1. Devote a whole departmental meeting to a particular aspect of teaching and learning. Review schemes of work, plan a new topic or moderate coursework.

2. Invite other people to join your departmental meeting such as the curriculum deputy, a governor or a local adviser.

3. Arrange a visit and plan how you can use a local resource more effectively, for example, a place of worship.

4. Visit the RE department at another secondary school. View their resources, hear about their different courses and generally share ideas.

5. Invite an outside speaker such as an examiner to attend your departmental meeting.

Managing Administration and Communications

All teachers have some administration to do but heads of department have a much heavier load. The key message is, not to allow yourself to become overwhelmed by administration. However, in order to succeed at this you need to adopt certain practices and strategies. These include:

1. Looking through your mail and quickly dividing it into information you will need to note, information you need to file or circulate, information for display and information that requires a response. This takes time so, if a response is needed, make a mental note. If at all possible, reply the same day. As is often said on management courses, 'don't handle the same piece of paper more than once'. Of course, this is not referring to everyday documents but to general administration. Deal with paper quickly: note, photocopy, file it or even 'bin' as appropriate.

2. Getting yourself a reputation for efficiency in responding quickly to memos and requests. But, also give yourself time to think and reflect if you are required to make a response to a critical memo. There can be a tendency to rush and say things in the wrong way.

3. Keeping the RE office or storage cupboard, well-organised. Filing trays, ring-binder files, documents, sections of notice boards should all be clearly labelled. There may be occasions when you are not in school and someone else should be able to find their way around your office. Confidential information should be locked away in files.

Ways of communicating more effectively

- As a head of department you will be communicating with other people for a range of purposes. Try to vary the formats and styles you adopt.

- You need to keep in touch with members of your team. An informal conversation over break-time may provide an opportunity to give dates of meetings but other information really needs to be written down and placed in pigeon-holes.

- Don't send lots of memos and notices where one would do. For example, if you are welcoming visitors into school, maybe this could go on the school bulletin.

- Technology is here to support working practices. If you are not computer literate and are not able to create memos and documents on the word processor, sign up for a course!

Managing a Budget

Schools have different strategies for allocating funding to curriculum departments. The first thing you must do is to establish just what the system is in your school. Sometimes teachers do not know the system and you should have access to this information. In addition to the departmental allocation, find out if there is a central fund for such items as stationery, photocopying and INSET courses. What about furnishings? In some schools, heads of department have to write out a bid presenting a case for certain resources. You will need to consider your aims and objectives for this particular sum of money. Be sure to relate these to school priorities and your departmental objectives and development plan.

Once you are clear what your funding is and how it has been arrived at, then you must spend time working on your budget. Plan well ahead so that when the new financial year begins, you are ready to place your orders. And remember that, in some schools, funding which is not spent by the end of the financial year is taken away. Don't let this happen in your RE department. While every teacher of RE would like a higher allocation of money, you have to manage with what you have been given. Consult your RE development plan. If you have costings as part of the plan, then your task will be much easier.

Before making any purchases, do 'check out' that it is really what is needed. Discuss with the RE team, see inspection copies of books, visit book shops, talk to other teachers or seek the advice of your local adviser. Ensure that you keep a careful account of what you have spent. An on-going file labelled 'budgets' would be useful. In many schools there is a bursar or finance officer who handles all the purchasing for you. This is a great help and it may be that you will receive a computerised departmental print-out. If not, be sure to check your records from time to time.

Departmental expenses

Bear the following in mind as you decide how to spend your budget:

- **Stationery:** Identify the supplies of folders, files, transparencies, exercise books, paper and display paper that you are likely to need;

- **Administrative costs:** Consider what percentage of the budget will be needed for photocopying and the production of materials;

- **Equipment:** Prioritise the item(s) you want to obtain over a number of years and balance cost against need in deciding which needs are the most pressing;

- **Accommodation and furnishings:** Consider the possible benefits of curtains, blinds, shelving, additional display boards, filing cabinets and frames for posters and pictures;

- **Book resources:** Decide whether to buy full class sets of new text books or purchase additional copies of current sets. Consider any new courses and examination needs. It is useful to be able to buy one copy of recently published RE text books for ideas and reference purposes. When making decisions check that you are considering pupils of all ages and abilities. Think about whether you should you be developing a classroom reference library;

- **Audio-visual resources:** Decide whether you are building up an effective video, slide and artefact collection. Check for each religion being studied that have you a wide range of materials including text books, resource books, background material for teachers, videos, photographs and artefacts;

- **Visits and visitors:** Make sure that the budget includes some money for this purpose. Remember to keep careful records including dates and costings;

- **INSET opportunities:** Keep a sum of money back for INSET courses and conferences;

- **Subscriptions to RE organisations:** Are you a member of the Christian Education Movement (CEM) and the Professional Council for RE (PCfRE)? It is strongly advised. However, if the school pays the subscription you have to leave all the resources behind when you move on to another school. Why not consider having a school and a personal subscription? The latter is tax deductible.

Discover other sources of funding

Sometimes there are local trusts which can provide a sum of money for an RE department or a particular project. If a trust does donate money to your department, as well as the obvious thank-you letter, invite a member of the trust to come into school and look around the department. Local faith groups may be willing to loan or donate artefacts, books and videos for use in RE lessons. Again, this can be very beneficial. They may need advice as to what to purchase so be prepared to spend time in discussion with them. Don't turn offers down. It may be that in one year the local Christian Church agrees to provide a set of Bibles or books on Christianity for the library. Even if Christian resources are not your priority for that particular year, take up the offer. Of course, you will be extremely grateful if resources are freely given to the RE department but it needs to be made clear to the school finance officer, if he or she hears about 'the gifts', that this generous giving should in no way reduce the amount of funding you are given.

Finally, evaluate at the end of each year how your budget has been spent and the effects of this. Sometimes purchases may have simply saved you time and energy but that in itself is good, so that your energy can be put elsewhere. Effective management of a budget should in time enhance the quality of teaching and learning in the classroom. It is also useful to get pupil feedback on the different kinds of resources you use.

Development Planning

Most school departments are now required to write a development plan. This is a useful tool which aims to ensure proper planning, delivery and evaluation of all aspects of a department. Over a period of time, an effective development plan helps teachers to manage, review and to implement good practice. So, how should an RE development plan be constructed?

It is usually the head of department who designs the RE development plan but it makes good sense to involve members of the department. The review of the RE development plan should be a regular agenda item at the departmental meeting. Anything can be included in the plan, provided it relates in some way to the work of the RE department. If your school has undergone a recent inspection, then there will probably be issues arising out of that process which need to be incorporated. Similarly, if the RE department has been visited by a local education authority adviser or a consultant, suggestions for review or future planning may well have been raised. In addition it is often the practice that departmental development plans should reflect the school development plan (SDP). So, for example, if there is a whole school focus on equal opportunities, or Assessment, Recording and Reporting, a department may be required to incorporate these issues into their plans. It can be interesting to see the different approaches taken by a range of departments in addressing the same issue.

There are dozens of models for development planning. You may have to follow a particular format in your school. If not, choose a format with which you feel you can work. It needs to be clear and straightforward but, in order to serve its purpose, should be specific and contain a reasonable amount of detail.

Your first task is to decide how many years will be 'covered' by your RE development plan. The frequent pattern is a five year span, broken down into short and long term targets. It is important to stress that the RE development plan is not a kind of 'wish list', nor is it a brainstorm of every single target imaginable or necessary to produce a superb RE department. Be realistic, select areas which appear relevant to the work of the department and prioritise these. Some will take longer to achieve than others. If urgent additional issues arise during the course of a year, your RE development plan can be amended. The two examples on the following pages, show how development plans can be structured. The first example (A) uses columns to define the nature of the task, those who are involved, the resources required, the criteria for success and the timetable for evaluation.

EXAMPLE A

TASKS AND TARGETS	WHO IS INVOLVED? WHO WILL BE RESPONSIBLE?	RESOURCES AND FUNDING NEEDED	SUCCESS CRITERIA AND DATE FOR EVALUATION
State the things to do, to aim for, to review, to implement. Number these, or use bullet points. Begin with short-term targets that you hope to achieve within a year or less. Then, build up to long-term targets. As an alternative, divide the column into boxes for each term.	*Consider here the people who will be directly involved. For example, the required action may involve the head of department, another teacher in the department or a member of the senior management team.*	*Think here about the 'cost' of the task or target in terms of staffing, budgets, materials and time.*	*Think how you know you will have achieved your target, including dates and deadlines.*

In example B, there is a page for each area and identical sub-headings are used on each page to cover the main area and focus, key issue(s), tasks and targets, implications for teachers, resources and funding and dates for review and evaluation.

EXAMPLE B

AREA OF FOCUS:	Decide which area or aspect of the department you wish to focus on, e.g. staffing, resourcing, teaching, learning, INSET, assessment, curriculum, public examinations, special educational needs or open evenings.
KEY ISSUES:	Consider if the area needs 'breaking down' to give a sharper focus. For example, 'learning' could be broken down into a particular key stage or a year group. Alternatively, learning could focus on improving learning opportunities across different year groups.
TASKS & TARGETS:	This is where you turn your key issue into *action*. What do you hope to do, aim for, review or implement?
IMPLICATIONS FOR TEACHING STAFF:	Consider here how teachers may be affected in both the short and long-term.

RESOURCES AND FUNDING:	Think how much of the RE funding will be required to carry out the task. Always give an estimate even if you do not know the precise cost.
TARGET DATE:	State a realistic time-scale to complete the task.
REVIEW DATE AND EVALUATION:	Once something has been achieved or implemented, you should decide when a review or evaluation would be appropriate. For example, an evaluation of new text books could be a short item at a department meeting. Other types of review may need to be considered over a longer period of time, such as the introduction of a new examination syllabus.

TYPICAL TASKS & TARGETS

The department intends to:

- review its marking system;
- increase opportunities for staff development;
- improve the range of learning strategies;
- review examination performance at GCSE and A Level;
- implement a system of visits to places of worship;
- compile a list of suitable visitors for use in RE lessons;
- raise the profile of RE around school;
- raise the profile of RE for different audiences;
- develop links with partner primary schools;
- increase specialist staffing;
- explore the greater use of information technology in RE;
- improve the take-up of examination courses;
- review RE's contribution to school open evenings;
- raise pupil achievement in specific year groups;
- make a contribution to collective worship;
- develop a class library;
- encourage pupils to make more effective use of the school library;
- improve the learning environment in RE classrooms;
- evaluate the current system of the storage and retrieval of RE resources;
- check that schemes of work are in line with syllabuses;
- enhance the quality of RE support from learning support assistants (LSAs);
- formulate new policies;
- update the departmental handbook;
- analyse the gender balance in classes and in examination results;
- develop more cross-curricular links;
- review the accessibility of resources to SEN pupils;
- consider ways of extending more-able pupils.

Section 11.
MARKETING RE

Keeping a high profile for RE amongst pupils, staff, parents and governors is an ongoing task. New teaching groups, changes in staffing and governing bodies and meetings with parents, are all a regular feature of school life. This section describes how marketing RE in your school must be a feature of your professional commitment to the subject.

Marketing to Pupils

You may be teaching in a flourishing department with 5% of curriculum time given to each year group, examination courses firmly established and a large well-appointed teaching room. If this is the case, you are very fortunate! Many RE teachers find they are still fighting for what numerous other departments have got already. Whatever your situation, you must never assume that the battle for RE has been won in your school. To state the obvious, all RE teachers must plan and deliver interesting lessons and mark pupils' work regularly. Conscientious, hard-working teachers are recognised by pupils.

Using displays

In order to ensure a high profile for RE, good displays are necessary not just in and outside the RE room but also around the school. You should check how display areas are allocated. Sometimes, different departments are responsible for different areas of the school. In other establishments, departments are offered a display area on rotation, often in the entrance hall. It is essential to create an 'RE culture' that gives the message 'RE is very much alive and developing in this school'. If there are several areas or corridors around the school currently looking rather drab, why not suggest display boards to senior management? There may be a special fund to carry out small improvements like this.

As pupils, staff or any school visitor approaches the RE area, then they should 'feel the RE presence'. Wonderful, eye-catching displays should attract their attention as they move into RE territory. Remember, displays can be valuable teaching aids. Teachers are rarely able to choose their own classrooms. If you have very unsatisfactory accommodation (compared to others) then this is something to raise with senior management at an appropriate moment. In the meantime, whatever your room is like, aim to make it a welcoming environment. For example, how about a notice 'Welcome to the RE room', or something similar. Pupils could even design a poster for you.

Without contravening health and safety regulations, utilise every available centimetre in your room. Go for maximum impact. Be adventurous - look at the ceiling, the walls, the different surfaces and surrounding cupboards and cabinets. Reflect how you will bring colour and vitality to this room. Overleaf are some of the types of displays to be found in and around RE classrooms. Don't forget to change your displays on a regular basis. Variety is the spice of life! Invest in clip frames to protect pupils' work.

Ideas for displays in the RE classroom

You could display:

- Pupils' written work including samples from different year groups;
- Models, artefacts and art work created by pupils;
- Posters and pictures about different religions and general pictures of nature;
- Artefacts from different religions, properly labelled;
- Large printed names of the religions being studied with an appropriate vocabulary list;
- Photographs of visits to different places, or visitors who have taken part in RE lessons;
- Informative wall charts, providing the structure of the courses you are currently exploring;
- Challenging, amusing sayings in speech bubbles;
- Holiday displays, travel brochures and leaflets relating to places with religious significance;
- Game displays designed by pupils;
- 'What is expected in RE?' - a large printed notice stating the aims and attainment targets for RE;
- Information on GCSE and A Level courses;
- 'Thoughts on RE' - some brief recent statements by years 10 and 11 about what they gained from RE lessons;
- Leaflets on 'the career value of RE';
- RE News-Board - encourage pupils to take responsibility for this. Ask colleagues and pupils to bring in items from newspapers and magazines relating to religious and moral issues;
- Activities/outings, visits arranged by the RE department;
- Details of RE competitions.

Even in schools where there is a successful RE department, it is necessary and helpful to remind pupils as to why they are doing RE. 'What's the use of RE, I'm not going to be a vicar?' is still a comment voiced in classrooms around the country. So, at the start of the school year, and without fail to pupils starting at secondary school in year 7, use part of your first RE lesson with the class to discuss why RE is taught in schools. Allow about 20-30 minutes for this exercise. You could begin by asking pupils their views but you will certainly need to be ready with your reasons. The summary sheet entitled 'What's the point of RE?' should be helpful to you. Either use it as a handout or write the key points on the blackboard before the lesson (rolling the board round so it can't be seen until the appropriate moment). Alternatively, devise your own handout which should link to the departmental aims in your handbook.

The summary can be used with most year groups, though if you are extending your discussion to 'What's the point of examination RE?' with older pupils you will need additional points relating to the chosen syllabus. Following discussion on 'What's the point of RE?' ensure pupils copy these reasons or stick them into the front of their exercise books. It is often helpful to refer back to these as the year progresses. Of course, it goes without saying that every RE lesson provides an opportunity for the marketing of RE.

WHAT'S THE POINT OF RE?

- It helps you understand the world in which you live. Both in Great Britain and throughout the world, millions of people practise a religion.

- It can help you to understand people you may meet, programmes you may see on television and magazines or books you may read. Much art, music and writing has been influenced by religious ideas.

- It encourages you to think about what you do and do not believe. You can't accept or reject something until you know about it.

- It helps you ask the right questions about important issues. For example, sometimes people can stop you on the street, talk to you about religion and may attempt to persuade you to believe. You need to know how to deal with this.

- The law requires the teaching of RE in schools. This has gone on for many years and the RE curriculum has been changed to make it more useful to you.

Marketing to Colleagues

Whatever kind of school you teach in there will, no doubt, be some colleagues who need enlightening about what happens in RE lessons. Some colleagues may themselves have experienced dull and boring RE lessons while others may feel strongly that school is not the right environment for learning about religion. You will never 'win over' every member of staff but you need to do everything you can to educate as many of them as possible. Unlike your RE lessons, conversing with colleagues may be a brief chat in the staff room or an after school conversation in the car park. Why are these conversations with staff so important? Simply because their views and advice to pupils could affect the RE department in a number of ways. For example: think about year 9 tutors giving advice about subject options, think about certain staff who sit on various committees and make curriculum decisions. It's worth taking every available opportunity to talk RE. Remember these points:

- **Talk informally to lots of colleagues:** Let it be known that the RE department is sociable, intelligent and has a sense of humour. Don't bore colleagues, but do share the occasional anecdote from your lessons.

- **Leave around the odd artefact, book, photo:** Of course, you just forgot to take them to your classroom but people are often fascinated and ask 'What's this?'.

- **Borrow from other departments:** Other subject areas can be very useful to you as a resource. Art may let you borrow slides/pictures of religious paintings and sculptures, Design & Technology could give you advice about the design and making of artefacts, Food (Technology) could help with a special focus on food in different religions and Music could loan instruments associated with different religions. If this happens, consider inviting colleagues to your RE room one lunch-time to see the display that results.

- **Ask for help:** When planning a visit out of school, select a teacher to accompany you who would really benefit and enjoy the experience.

- **Volunteer your services** for different school working parties and committees. Yes, this will be more work but it's a great way to get to know other staff and play a key part in important discussions.

- **Maintain effective relationships** with colleagues and the members of the senior management team because they frequently make decisions which may affect departments.

Marketing to Governors

Governors are key people within a school community. If you are teaching in a church school, then almost certainly some governors will have a strong link with RE - they may have helped to appoint you and have firm views on the subject. You should try and secure good working relationships with them. In county schools, each member of the governing body is sometimes linked to a particular curriculum department. Other schools have a more casual arrangement. Ask if a governor can be linked to the RE department. The obvious choice, a local vicar, may not always be the best candidate but this person can be a useful strategic voice for RE among the rest of the governing body. Depending on how much time and energy your governor has, consider inviting him or her to be involved in some of the following activities:

- visiting lessons;
- reading through your departmental handbook;
- joining a departmental meeting;
- accompanying you on an RE visit;
- meeting with you to learn about the approach to RE;
- looking at a range of pupils' work.

In some schools, heads of department are asked to give a presentation to governors. If you are offered this opportunity, seize it. It's surprising how much you can get across in a brief talk with accompanying transparencies, handouts and a small display. If this system does not operate in your school, why not suggest it? Keep in regular contact with your 'link' governor. You never know when you might need their support.

Marketing to Parents

Hopefully, many parents will come to understand what RE is about through looking at their children's books or through chatting with them. However, you cannot depend on this happening, so you need to consider how you can raise the profile of RE amongst parents. Some parents are unsure of the value of RE with particular reference to examination courses. It's up to you to convince them. The following suggestions may be helpful in marketing RE to parents:

- Setting interesting homework which engages pupils in worthwhile research and assignments;
- Writing informative, accurate reports;
- Marking pupils' work thoroughly and carefully;
- Organising an RE open evening where parents can visit, talk to you, ask questions and see the resources that are available.

Also, be high profile on options evenings. Set out your RE stall with relevant literature, including a handout about the career value of RE. Older pupils could be available to share their views on RE, samples of pupils' coursework and copies of examination syllabuses and papers are all useful.

Other tactics can prove popular in marshalling support. Invite parents to accompany pupils and yourself on a visit to a place of worship. Aim to reach parents in year 7 first. If they have a good experience this can help the status of RE. Also, invite parents with particular skills or interests into RE lessons to make a contribution though it will probably not be a good idea to invite the father of a year 8 pupil into the class where his child is a pupil.

Marketing to the Local Community

Whether or not your school has a religious foundation, it serves a community of people that includes members of religious groups. Aim to find out which faith groups are represented in your area. Start compiling a list. It takes time and effort to build links but it is worth it and these groups can be a useful resource. Again, some may need enlightening about current developments in RE but who better to tell them than you? Also, enquire about charitable organisations, hospices and care groups in your locality. Some of these may be relevant to your RE curriculum.

Consider organising a lunch or after school event for representatives of different faith groups. Discuss this with your headteacher because such occasions can be very positive for the school. Don't be over ambitious, but design a short programme including a meeting with your Headteacher, a brief talk by RE Department, a tour of the school and a look at RE resources. Begin or finish with refreshments. Why not invite the local paper to come and take a picture? It's good publicity for the school and raises the profile of RE.

Ways to enhance links with local faith groups and organisations

1. Design a brief handout which describes the content and approach to RE in your school. Ensure the reader of a welcome if they decide to visit. State how you can be contacted.
2. Write to different groups/organisations offering your services as someone who can talk to them about RE.
3. When you have secured your contacts, ask if faith groups would like to donate artefacts or books to the school. If these are instructional as opposed to educational materials, that does not matter since you can show pupils the sort of literature communities use to nurture the faith in their members.

Section 12.
STAFF DEVELOPMENT

Continuous professional development is an entitlement for all staff and it is important for any department to seek out opportunities for its teachers. This section explores this area as well as considering the appointment and promotion of new staff.

Local Support for RE

All education authorities have a SACRE (Standing Advisory Council for RE). This group can offer support to RE teachers, so find out the membership of your local SACRE. If your school is under local authority control, then there may be other support services available. Your school could be entitled to these by right or it may be that some services have to be purchased either as you use them, or through an annual subscription. Check out this procedure with your school.

Most local authorities have appointed an individual with responsibility for RE. This could be an inspector, an adviser or an advisory teacher. Aim to make contact with this person as soon as you start at your school. Keep their name, office address, and a contact number in your diary. You never know when you might need their services! Although different local authorities operate in different ways, it is well worth exploring what your local expert can do for you.

How an adviser can help

Ask your adviser for help on:

- OFSTED inspection;
- pre-inspection and post-inspection support;
- reviewing and monitoring of the RE department;
- handling newly qualified teachers (NQT);
- providing RE INSET in and outside school;
- speaking to governors about the RE curriculum;
- finding new resources;
- establishing new courses;
- attending interviews for RE posts;
- professional matters and job references;
- local networking;
- presenting RE issues to the headteacher or senior managers;
- clarifying legal requirements;
- coursework moderation.

Do not assume that the local education authority adviser will be able to carry out any task. Like anyone else, he or she will have their own workload which will include responsibility for many schools. However, do find out what kind of support you can realistically expect. If your school is not under local education authority control, you may still be able to 'buy-in' to the local education authority service or, as an alternative, form links with an RE consultant. There are many consultants across the country but it is wise to 'check out' their credentials before your school pays any fee. Consultants often work independently but they may be 'attached' to a higher education establishment such as a university department of education or to a diocese.

Alternatively, you may be teaching in a school with a religious foundation - Christian (Catholic, Church of England), Jewish or Muslim. There are usually specific people who have the responsibility to support RE in these schools. Your headteacher will probably put you in touch with the designated person from the relevant religious group.

Through making this kind of contact you will probably find that RE courses may be organised on a local basis. Always ask to receive information about RE INSET and, when the subject matter is relevant, do attend a course. Not only will this enhance your professional RE development but it also provides a wonderful opportunity of meeting colleagues from other schools. It is important for the department to keep a record of INSET attended by different teachers. A simple system can operate whereby anyone who has attended a course fills in a form which is then filed in the department. Over time, a useful record can then be built up. Also, find ways of disseminating what you have learnt to other members of the department, maybe at a departmental meeting.

A Typical INSET profile

NAME:	COURSE TITLE:
DATE:	VENUE:
PROVIDER:	COST:
KEY FACTORS IDENTIFIED:	
IMPLICATIONS FOR SCHOOL AND POSSIBLE ACTION:	
EVALUATION REQUIRED:	

National Groups and Organisations

There are many national groups concerned with religious education. It is not possible to mention all of them but the following information will enable you as a professional RE teacher to know about some of the key organisations and what they do. Their addresses are provided in the *Resource Guide*.

SCAA (School Curriculum and Assessment Authority) has a responsibility for monitoring the national curriculum and religious education. Its publications include the Model Syllabuses for RE, a glossary of religious terms, an annual analysis of SACRE reports, GCSE, A Level and AS Level examination results and various discussion papers relating to spiritual, moral, social and cultural development. SCAA has a Professional Officer for RE. The authority has merged with the NCVQ (National Council for Vocational Qualifications) in 1997 to form the Qualifications and Curriculum Authority (QCA).

AREIAC (Association of Religions Education Inspectors, Advisers and Consultants) represents all those whose professional responsibilities involve them in advising SACREs, local authorities and schools in relation to RE and collective worship, or who inspect RE and collective worship.

The Culham Institute is a research, development and information agency working in the fields of church schools, church colleges and religious education. It works with other trusts and organisations to produce support for RE teachers through a range of materials and through sponsoring conferences, seminars and in-service training relating to RE. The Institute manages the Sir Halley Stewart Teacher Fellowship for RE teachers.

RE-XS (Religious Education Exchange Service) is designed for use by all who are involved in the teaching and learning of Religious and Moral Education whether in an official or personal capacity and regardless of age and educational level. The service is in two sections: the first provides a directory of on-line resources and the second gives access to interactive tools.

NASACRE (National Association of SACREs) assists members of local SACREs to fulfil their responsibilities and seeks to liaise with other agencies as appropriate. National conferences are organised and a newsletter is published.

SHAP was formed following a conference held near Shap (in the Lake District) in 1969 for those interested in the development of world religions in education. Participants came from a variety of religious backgrounds and represented all phases of education. A working party on world religions in education emerged. SHAP organises conferences and produces publications, including an annual calendar of religious festivals.

RESPECT is a termly journal for teachers of RE to pupils of all abilities at key stages 1-3. Through articles and examples of good practice, the journal aims to support busy teachers in helping pupils learn about world religions in line with County Agreed Syllabuses and the SCAA Model Syllabus for RE. A wide range of resources are also available.

CEM (Christian Education Movement) is an ecumenical educational charity which supports religious and moral education in schools. It is committed to the teaching of the major world faiths in RE and to an accurate and fair representation of their beliefs and practices in all its teaching materials. It publishes teaching materials and papers, including the magazine *RE Today*, *Resource* and the *British Journal of Religious Education*. It also offers a range of other services. This is the national organisation to which most secondary RE teachers belong.

PCfRE (Professional Council for RE) is a professional association for those who teach RE providing a focal point for their concerns and a representative voice at national level.

The Farmington Institute for Christian Studies was founded to support and improve Christian education. It is ecumenical in its commitment to the Christian faith and is keen to develop good relations with other world religions. Work in the field of RE includes the publication of Farmington Papers (of interest to sixth form teachers of RE) and an annual prize for an outstanding RE department in a secondary school. One term Farmington Fellowships are awarded to secondary RE teachers for a term of study at a specified university or college. The costs of college fees and a replacement teacher are covered by the institute.

The Religious Education Council is an independent body comprised of a wide range of faith communities and nationally representative professional RE teacher associations. It meets regularly to consider matters affecting RE in schools and is concerned with the promotion of RE at a national level.

The Association of Christian Teachers (ACT) provides a wide range of classroom materials, INSET for teachers, including distance learning courses validated by Nottingham University. ACT and Stapleford House will ultimately form into two separate charities. Stapleford House will become the Stapleford Institute and will be responsible for providing INSET (including the distance learning course) and RE resources.

The Catholic Education Service is the education agency of the Catholic Bishops' Conference and acts as an advisory body on all matters affecting Catholic primary and secondary schools and colleges of further and higher education.

The Free Church Federal Council is the voice for free churches in public education with nineteen member denominations. There is an education committee with special concern for religious, moral, spiritual education and support for its members elected on to SACREs.

The Church of England's Board of Education is the official voice of the Church of England on Education. It works for schools, in close conjunction with the National Society. This is a voluntary Anglican body which is responsible for a large RE Centre in London. It provides courses for teachers, denominational inspections and general information on all aspects of RE.

The Inter-Faith Network for the United Kingdom was set up by people of all faiths and now links the major faith communities in Britain and promotes good relations between them. There are eighty member organisations, including representative bodies from the faith communities, local inter-faith groups, academic institutions and bodies concerned with multi-faith education.

The Buddhist Society provides information and advice. There are also lectures and seminars.

The British Sikh Education Council provides information, a range of publications and organises conferences.

The Hindu Council of Birmingham is a contact point for requesting information about local Hindu organisations in other areas.

The Muslim Educational Trust advises on the educational needs of Muslim children and produces a range of publications.

The Board of Deputies of British Jews through its education department provides a means of obtaining information on most aspects of Judaism whether required by secondary school pupils, university students or teachers. Answers to specific questions, book-lists, and the addresses of bookshops and artefact shops can be sent. Visits to schools by speakers and day tours of Jewish London can be arranged by request.

Contact addresses are contained in the *Resource Guide*. Specifically for independent schools, the Independent Schools' Religious Studies Association publishes a newsletter, *The Independent Schools Religious Studies Association Newsletter and Journal*, while *The Chaplains' Encyclical* is a newsletter for chaplains, reporting on good practice, including that in religious studies.

Applications and Interviews

Whether or not you are planning to apply for a new post in the immediate future, it is always useful to have your curriculum vitae (CV) in an up-to-date word-processed form. Most teaching posts are advertised in the *Times Educational Supplement*. There is never a great deal of time to spare in getting an application together, so you need to move quickly once you see a job that interests you. Either ring the school or write off for details. You will probably be required to send a large s.a.e. so always have a few in store. Once you receive details, read the information carefully and make the decision whether or not you want to apply. Sometimes a conversation with a respected colleague in your school can be helpful. If you decide to apply, inform your headteacher and request a reference should your application be taken up. Consider too who you will choose for your second referee.

The information pack will tell you how to apply. Often it will be by filling in an application form so make sure you try a rough draft first. You may be asked to write a letter as to your reasons for applying for this particular post. Aim for an average length of letter. If it is several pages long or perhaps only a paragraph, your form may be discarded. The purpose of your application is to excite the readers at the other end and to indicate your suitability for this particular post. An effective letter of application should produce an interview.

Getting an interview

- Ensure that your letter of application matches (as far as it can) the details set out in the job description/specification. Use the information they have sent you.

- Don't oversell yourself, giving credit for areas in which you have little or no experience.

- Be realistic and honest. If a school requires someone to teach philosophy and ethics at A Level and you have no experience, say so. However, do convince them that you have the ability, enthusiasm, skill and dynamism to prepare and deliver an excellent course.

- Always keep a copy of the application form and the job details. This is vital in case you are called for interview - you can then recall exactly what you said. Also, it is helpful to look back at unsuccessful applications as you consider other posts in the future.

- It may be that the school has not asked for a CV but if yours contains important information which you have not managed to mention in the letter or on the application form, you could send one. A CV should be word-processed or typed.

Preparing for an interview

If you are invited for an interview, confirm with the school that you will attend. Inform your headteacher that you have an interview and ask for the day off school. Plan your travel arrangements, giving yourself ample time to make the journey. If the school is not too far away it may be worth making a visit the week-end prior to the interview so that you know the exact location and get 'the feel of the place'. Re-read your letter of application and all the information sent to you.

You may be asked to teach a lesson or make a short presentation. You must prepare this thoroughly. If you are requested to teach a lesson, write a lesson plan, photocopy and have it ready to hand to your observer(s) on the day. Think in advance of any materials you will need. The school will probably provide these if you let them know. Take anything else with you which might enhance your lesson such as pictures or artefacts.

Make a list of questions which need answering on the day of interview. These may be RE specific or quite general. Some could well be answered as you look around the school and chat informally. If not, it is quite acceptable to ask questions during the interview. If you think you might forget, jot them down in a notebook. You may like to ask a senior colleague to give you a practice interview beforehand.

As you look around the school and meet people, try and look relaxed, smile and keep your eyes open for interesting displays of work, or activities. Sometimes the formal interview process might begin with the question: 'You've had time to look around the school, what has impressed you, what do you think about our buildings?'

The interview process

Generally you will be interviewed by a panel - the headteacher, a member of staff (depending on what kind of post this is, e.g. head of RE or main scale RE teacher), and a governor. You will be introduced to the panel at the start of the interview. Try and look relaxed but not too laid back, and endeavour to make eye contact with all the panel as you are speaking.

Questions will be many and varied so if you are not absolutely clear about the meaning of a question, ask politely for a rephrase. It is not always easy to sense what can be an adequate length of answer. It is perfectly acceptable to say 'I can elaborate my answer further if you would like that'. You will probably be asked at the start or at the end of the interview, whether or not you are still interested in the post. Be prepared for this question. After the interview, candidates may be sent home and told to wait for a phone call or asked to remain until a decision has been reached.

Appointing a Second RE Teacher in Your Department

As head of department you should be part of the important process of selecting a new RE teacher. Hopefully, you will be involved in all three stages of the process that begins long before the appointment is made. The first stage involves scheduling the process, the preparation of a job description or specification, and the design of an advertisement. The next stage is the reading of applications and short-listing of candidates for reference. Then, on the day of interview you will be looking after candidates and showing them around the RE department before acting as a member of the interview panel.

Stage 1 - Before the interviews

The job description and specification: the first question to ask is what kind of person are you looking for? What strengths and expertise are needed in the department? What new areas could be developed by the right candidate? To help you write the job description ask yourself about:

- the job title;
- the teaching allocation;
- the religions you would like taught;
- other possible responsibilities such as co-ordinator for KS3, non examination courses or displays you would like to include.

Devise a personal specification based on your answers. The areas you cover should include:

- **Qualifications:** Will you expect a degree, a diploma in specific areas or qualifications in religious studies or theology?
- **Experience:** Are you seeking a newly qualified teacher or one with several years teaching?
- **Special requirements:** Are you looking for the ability to work in a team or a willingness to be a form tutor? Is there a requirement to teach a second subject?

This specification - or a version of it like that overleaf - will normally be sent to applicants so remember that they are the target audience. The next stage is to devise the advertisement. Keep it brief, aim to attract candidates to apply and summarise the information in the job description and specification.

A typical job description for second in the RE department

This is a new post in the school. The timetable will be largely RE with the possibility of a few lessons of a second subject. The post-holder will be responsible to the head of RE in assisting with the running of the department.

Specific Duties

To assist the head of RE in delivering the RE curriculum throughout the school.
To be responsible for RE displays throughout the school.
From time to time, carry out additional duties as directed by the headteacher.

General Duties

Adhere to the equal opportunities policy of the school.
Attend staff and department meetings as required.
Take on the responsibility of a tutor group.

These duties are to be reviewed and revised as and when appropriate.

A typical advertisement

Required for September 1998 a teacher (CPS) to assist in the RE department.

A well qualified and enthusiastic teacher is needed for this amply resourced and successful department. The post would involve teaching up to GCSE level with the possibility of some general RE in the sixth form. Newly qualified teachers are invited to apply along with those who have some experience in RE teaching.

Application forms and further details can be obtained from the headteacher at the school and should be returned within 14 days of this advertisement.

A typical job specification

TITLE: Second in RE department

GRADE: Main Scale CPS

ATTRIBUTES	ESSENTIAL	DESIRABLE
QUALIFICATIONS	1. Graduate - degree or equivalent in theology, RE, RS or related discipline. 2. Teaching qualification.	• Content of degree to include Christianity. • Knowledge of other religions.
EXPERIENCE	3. Experience of teaching RE across KS3 and KS4. 4. Experience of teaching Christianity and some other religions. 5. Ability to enthuse pupils about RE.	• Experience of Sixth form general RE. • Experience of GCSE RE/RS • Knowledge and experience of multicultural environment.
SKILLS	6. Ability and interest in promoting RE through effective displays. 7. Effective communication and organisational skills.	• Computer literacy.
MOTIVATION AND POTENTIAL	8. Ability and willingness to work within a small department. 9. Willingness to teach a second subject.	• Willingness to be involved in liaising with faith communities. • Interest in professional development through conferences and courses.
SPECIAL REQUIREMENTS		

Sorting the applications: Don't expect to have full control over this area of the process. It is commonly a task shared between headteacher and head of department but often a local adviser will also be involved. As you read applications, mentally note the organisation and presentation of material. Keep the job description and personal specification in front of you. Designing a simple checklist will help to ensure that all candidates are treated fairly.

Once the references have arrived, check the referees' statements against each candidate's application and the requirements of the job. Try to read 'between the lines'. An honest reference will refer to weaknesses as well as strengths. All candidates should have cited their present headteacher as one referee or explained why they have not. Agree a short-list with your headteacher of up to six candidates and keep some names in reserve in case of late withdrawals.

It is likely to be your job to inform the candidates about the department. Provide them with basic information about the RE department, the staff and the facilities as well as an outline syllabus in an information pack. Make the departmental handbook available on the interview day. Let them know the programme for the day and make it clear if they are expected to teach a lesson or give a presentation. If so, give them details of the class including age, ability and the current syllabus topic. Remember that any covering letter should be welcoming and ask for confirmation of attendance.

Stage 2 - The day of the interviews

It is vital that a number of people, but especially you as head of RE, spend plenty of time with candidates so that a good decision is made. So, it is worth spending time showing candidates around and answering their questions. As you do this, you should find out a lot about them as well.

Introduce candidates to other teachers who are connected to the RE department including non-specialists and humanities teachers in adjacent rooms. Their feedback may be useful later in the day as will a brief chat with each candidate prior to the formal interview.

If candidates are asked to teach a lesson, use a standard form to note how they react to totally new pupils and how pupils respond to them. If you are not involved in the formal interview and, sadly, that is sometimes the case, then giving clear feedback to the headteacher before the formal interviews is vital. Assuming that you are a member of the interview panel you will need to meet for a briefing session before the formal interview. The headteacher or a senior governor usually chairs the interview and will suggest the procedure. Have a bank of questions ready. You may have to adapt your questions if, say, the governor representative decides to ask 'one of yours' or if some areas have already been thoroughly explored during informal conversations.

All candidates should be asked similar questions. There can, of course, be additional questions if clarification is needed. It is essential that as candidates are asked questions, notes are kept by the panel. In the decision-making process, expect other members of the panel to consult you about the subject expertise of candidates and make your case clearly if you feel that some are stronger than others. At the same time, recognise that the other members may perceive the overriding needs of the school differently from your subject perspective. Once a decision has been made, book a time for your new member of the department to visit either before he or she leaves or shortly afterwards.

Typical interview questions

Questions about personal values and professional skill:

- Talk about an RE lesson recently taught that has gone well. Explain why.
- How did you feel about the lesson you taught this morning? (When candidates are asked to teach as part of the interview.)
- Could you outline the professional and personal qualities you have which make you a strong candidate for this post?
- Would you be willing to lead an extra curricular club such as a Christian Union, although it is not part of the job description?
- What are your views on the RE department making occasional contributions to collective worship?
- What do you understand the terms 'spiritual and moral development' to mean?
- Do you think it is important for an RE teacher to be a religious believer?
- What particular strengths do you feel you can bring to this school through teaching RE?
- Having read about and seen the RE department, could you outline your vision for RE in this school?

Questions about the role of RE in the school:

- How would you respond to a pupil who asks 'Why do we have to do RE?'?
- How would you respond to a parent at a Parents' Evening who asks 'Why does my daughter have to learn about so many religions? Why not just concentrate on Christianity?'?
- Imagine it is an Open Evening and the RE classroom will be open to visitors. How would you organise your room?
- How will you ensure that pupils with special needs are fully involved in RE lessons?
- In this school few pupils belong to any particular religious group. How will you attempt to interest them all in RE?
- How does RE contribute to multicultural education?
- How could you raise the profile of RE within a school?
- What is your view on homework in RE?
- How will you develop information technology through the RE curriculum?
- Do you see RE linking with other areas of the curriculum?
- What are the distinctive features of an effective RE department?
- How does RE contribute to pupils' spiritual, moral, social and cultural development?
- How would you raise the awareness of the European dimension in the RE curriculum?
- How will you support the several non-specialist teachers who are involved in teaching RE?
- How would you monitor the quality of RE teaching and learning within the RE department?
- What strategies might you suggest in order to improve examination results at GCSE and A Level?
- How would you make decisions about what kind of syllabus to teach at A Level?

Questions about the subject:

- Is differentiation a possibility for RE teachers when so many pupils and classes are seen only once a week?
- What are your views on the SCAA Model Syllabuses for RE?
- What would be your ideal solution for teaching RE at KS4?
- What do you consider to be your main aims in RE for all pupils?
- Can you describe what you would expect a religiously educated 16-year-old to be like?
- How will you make a decision about which religions to teach in RE?
- Can you describe how RE has changed and developed in the last ten years?
- What recent INSET courses have you attended and how have they helped you?
- Can you suggest any excellent RE resources you have used recently and explain why you consider them to be excellent?
- What are some of the key issues facing the professional RE teacher?
- What kinds of areas are being assessed in RE?

An evaluation grid for assessing applications and drawing up a short-list

POST:	CANDIDATES				
Assistant in RE Dept	1	2	3	4	5
• Graduate/equivalent in theology RS/RE/related field.					
• Teaching qualification and skills.					
• Competency in teaching about world religions.					
• Experience of teaching world religions.					
• Experience of teaching RE across KS3 and KS4.					
• Experience of teaching GCSE RE/RS.					
• Experience of teaching sixth form general RE.					
• Experience of multicultural environment.					
• Ability and motivation to create effective RE displays.					
• Competence and willingness to teach a second subject.					
• Computer literacy.					
• Experience of working in a small department.					
• Evidence of willingness to be involved with different faith groups.					
• Evidence of professional development through conferences, INSET, etc.					
• Evidence of participation in extra curricular activities.					
Totals scored by each candidate. Maximum for each - 5.					

Section 13.
STAFF DEVELOPMENT ACTIVITIES

This section provides three photocopiable discussion activities for use with staff and other groups that are central to the work of any RE department.

INSET ACTIVITY ONE: Aims in Religious Education

Use this checklist with teachers, parents, governors and older pupils. Ask individuals to identify five priorities from the list and then share them with, first another person, then a small group of four and then with a larger group so that agreement and consensus is developed as the discussion goes on.

In the larger group, raise these questions:-

- **Which of these aims are unique to RE?**
- **Are any of these aims contrary to what you think RE should be doing?**
- **Are any of these aims unprofessional?**
- **Does RE help to develop pupils in a unique way?**

RE should aim to:

1. educate pupils for the world in which they live: people need to be religiously literate to live in the modern world;
2. help pupils understand their multicultural and multi-faith society;
3. encourage pupils to understand a religion from the point of view of a believer;
4. make pupils practising Christians;
5. help pupils reflect upon their experiences and confront 'ultimate questions';
6. expand ways of looking at the world and promote a world-wide consciousness;
7. give pupils the skills to make judgements between conflicting beliefs and values;
8. enable pupils to understand the nature of religious beliefs and practices;
9. teach morality;
10. teach tolerance towards people of different faiths;
11. enable pupils to understand the importance and influence of religious beliefs and practices in the lives of believers;
12. encourage pupils to search for truth;
13. help pupils to understand the foundations upon which some of the world's great civilisations have been built;
14. reflect on and respond to the spiritual dimension of life;
15. help pupils in their own personal search for meaning;
16. help pupils better understand their culture and its art and literature;
17. teach pupils how to use religious language;
18. enable pupils to think religiously and to be religiously literate;
19. explore other world views, including non-religious stances in life such as secularism or humanism;
20. help pupils recognise their own 'tacit religion';
21. bring pupils into an encounter with Jesus Christ;
22. help pupils discuss personal and social issues;
23. help pupils come to a belief in God;
24. educate pupils in the religious heritage of their country;
25. teach pupils the difference between right and wrong.

Some further issues to consider with subject specialists:-
- **What is the relationship between learning about religion and learning from religion?**
- **How are pupils to learn from a religion without being indoctrinated into a religion?**

INSET ACTIVITY TWO: Teaching World Religions

Use these materials to guide a discussion of how you teach world religions with colleagues, parents, representatives of faith groups and interested outsiders.

The SCAA Model Syllabuses identify six principal religions. Individual Agreed Syllabuses may well specify which ones to cover, but the teacher may be left with a choice. When choosing which religion to study consider:

- **the backgrounds of your pupils;**
- **the requirements of the syllabus you are following;**
- **teacher expertise;**
- **resource implications;**
- **links with local community;**
- **the balance of time you spend on any one religion.**

Next, consider these key points in discussing your approach:

- A religion should be approached as an integrated way of life that presents a view of the world;
- Care should be taken to treat each religion as a world view and not to be too selective in the choice of material. For example, it would be wrong to teach Judaism only from the point of view of Reform Judaism, or Buddhism from the point of view of Mahayana Buddhism. Breadth and balance are key concepts;
- A religion should be treated as a world religion and the variety of religious expression within a religion underlined;
- Pupils should be allowed to understand and explore the truth claims of a religion since the adherents of religions make claims about the world and their beliefs which they consider to be objectively true.

Finally, consider these points as a guide to classroom activity:

- Treat each religion as a living faith. Aim to bring the faith alive in the classroom by using primary evidence wherever possible so, for example, let Hindus speak for Hinduism through quotes, videos and visits;
- Use a variety of resources to bring alive the religion - music, smells and tastes (for example, food or incense), art work and videos, visits and visitors;
- Do not treat world religions as spiritual supermarkets from which pupils can choose a belief here, a skill there, a virtue from this religion and an attitude from another;
- Relate any religious material to the world of the pupil so that there are points of contact.

INSET ACTIVITY THREE: Promoting Spiritual and Moral Development

This activity allows a department or group of interested teachers to consider how to promote the spiritual, moral, social and cultural (SMSC) development of pupils.

The checklist below identifies some ways in which the spiritual, moral, social and cultural development of pupils can be promoted. As you discuss each item, provide examples of units of work which could enable you to explore them in the classroom.

It is possible to support SMSC development by encouraging pupils to:

- consider life's fundamental questions;
- value elements of human existence which are not provable;
- express their thoughts and feelings about their relation to the world and other people;
- reflect on spiritual issues;
- explore music, art and world literature;
- develop a sense of right and wrong;
- examine their motives for action;
- develop decision-making skills and use these to examine a variety of moral issues;
- examine religious rules and codes of ethics;
- explore links between beliefs and values;
- consider the need for consistency between beliefs and actions;
- challenge hypocrisy;
- examine moral language and its use;
- show consideration towards others;
- show awareness of the needs of others;
- promote honesty and integrity;
- discuss ethical issues about the self, relationships with others and societal issues;
- take personal responsibility for their own actions;
- explore the consequences of behaviour;
- consider issues of evil and suffering;
- formulate and review their own values;
- treat one another courteously and respectfully;
- reflect on moral absolutes;
- engage in moral behaviour;
- consider the different social groups in society;
- talk about roles and responsibilities;
- explore the relationship between the individual citizen and society;
- understand a variety of cultures;
- explore the relationship between religion and culture;
- explore how other cultures seek a spiritual dimension to life;
- explore how religious ideas are expressed in different cultural settings such as art, music and literature.

THE RESOURCE GUIDE

Any list of resources is inevitably selective. This section offers a wider range of quality resources and contacts than a set of book references, including publishers, national organisations concerned with RE, teacher centres and suppliers of religious artefacts.

Book publishers

Addison, Wesley,
Longman
Fourth Avenue
Harlow
Essex
CM19 5AA

Bible Society
Stonehill Green
Westlea
Swindon
SN5 7DG

Blackwell Education
Marston Book Services
PO Box 87
Osney Mead
Oxford
OX2 0DT

Cambridge University
Press
The Edinburgh Building
Cambridge
CB2 1BR

Cassell, Chapman,
Mowbray
Stanley House
3 Fleets Lane
Poole
Dorset
BH15 3AJ

Christian Education
Movement
Royal Buildings
Victoria Street
Derby
DE1 1GW

Collins Educational
Harper Collins
Publishers
Westerhill Road
Bishopsbriggs
Glasgow
G64 1BR

Heinemann Educational
Halley Court
Jordan Hill
Oxford

Hodder and Stoughton
Direct Services
Abingdon
Oxfordshire
OX14 4YY

Lion Publishing
Freepost
St Peter's Way
Sandy Lane West
Oxford
OX4 5BR

Macmillan Education
Houndsmill
Basingstoke
Hampshire
RG21 2XS

Monarch Publications
PO Box 163
Tunbridge Wells
Kent
TN3 0NZ

Thomas Nelson
North Way
Andover
Hampshire
SP10 5BR

Oxford University
Press
Walton Street
Oxford
OX2 6DP

RMEP
St Mary's Works
St Mary's Plain
Norfolk
NR3 3BH

RESPECT
7 Elyham
Purley-on-Thames
Pangbourne
Berkshire
RG8 8EN

Stanley Thornes
Freepost (GR782)
Cheltenham
Gloucester
GL50 1BR

Published key texts linked to approaches to the subject

The Phenomenological Approach

Religions, Longman (1988)
Skills in RE, Heinemann (1989)
Examining Religions Series, Heinemann (1989)
Believers in One God; Seekers of Religion, Cambridge University Press (1993)

The Experiential Approach

New Methods in RE Teaching: An Experiential Approach, Oliver and Boyd (1990)

The Conceptual Approach

Key Christian Beliefs, Lion Publishing, (1995)
Life Issues, Lion Publishing (1997)
TOOLKIT, Bible Society
Religion For Today Series, Oxford University Press (1996)

The Thematic Approach

Living Questions, Stanley Thornes (1993)
Religion for a Change, Stanley Thornes

The Ethnographic Approach

Interpreting Religions Series, Heinemann (1995)

Collections of stories

Canfield J & Hansen M V, *Chicken Soup for the Soul: 101 stories to open the heart and rekindle the spirit*, Health Communications Inc., Florida (1993)

de Mello A, *The Song of the Bird*, Gujarat Sahitya Prakash

de Mello A, *One Minute Wisdom*, Image Books

de Mello A, *The Prayer of the Frog*, Gujarat Sahitya Prakash

de Mello A, *The Heart of the Enlightened*, Collins

de Mello A, *One Minute Nonsense*, Gujarat Sahitya Prakash

Lefevre P, *One Hundred Stories to Change Your Life*, St Paul Publications

Wood A & Richardson R, *Inside Stories: Wisdom and Hope for Changing Worlds*, Trentham Books (1992)

Information on religions in the UK

Information on religions in the UK can be found in an extensive handbook entitled *Religions in the UK* published jointly by the University of Derby and the Inter-Faith Network. The 1997 edition is available from:
The Religious Resource and Research Centre
University of Derby
Mickleover
Derby
DE3 5GX
Tel: 01332 622222 Ext. 2102.
Fax: 01332 514323

Artefacts

Buddhism

Buddha rupa (image of the Buddha)
Chorten or stupa (originally a burial mound)
Dorje
Bell

Incense holder
Tibetan prayer wheel
Tapes of Buddhist chants
Wesak cards

Christianity

Christmas
Advent calendar
Advent candle
Christmas tree decorations
Small box, gift wrapped
Christmas cards - both secular and religious
Christingle
St Lucia head garland
Christmas carol sheet
Posters showing Christmas celebrations around the world
Nativity scene or crib figures
Tapes of Christmas music
Statue of Madonna and child

Easter
Easter cards
Palm crosses
Variety of crosses - crucifix, empty cross
Easter egg boxes
An Easter garden
Tapes of Easter music

Easter candles
Posters showing Easter celebrations around the world
Pictures of stations of the cross
Decorated eggs

General
Bibles in various translations
Service Book (Book of Common Prayer; Alternative Service Book)
Bible study notes
Baptism candle
Cards: for Baptism, Believer's Baptism, Dedication, Confirmation

Certificates: for, Baptism, Communion, Confirmation, Dedication
Communion cup
Communion Paten
Fish badge stickers
Rosary
Tapes: different styles of music (e.g. Taize)
Icon

Hinduism

Images: Hindu deities
Models or pictures of temples/shrines
Puja set
Aarti lamp
Hindu comic books
Prayer beads
Deva lamp

Diva incense sticks
Divali cards
Garland for festivities
OM sign (symbol for God as badge or sticker)
Tape of Indian music

Islam

Prayer mat
Prayer beads (tasbir)
Qur'an
Qur'an stand
Calligraphic texts

Compass (to tell the direction of Mecca)
Festival cards: e.g. Eid card
Kaaba - as a picture or model
Prayer hat

Judaism

Tallit (prayer shawl)
Yamulkah, Capel, Kepah (skull cap)
Tefillin (prayers which are contained in
a box on the forehead and arm)
Shabbat candles
Challot cover (to cover the challot
bread on Shabbat)
Candlesticks
Kiddush cup (for the wine used on
Shabbat)
Havdalah candle (the candle used at
the end of Shabbat) and spice box
Seder plate (for Passover)
Haggadah (service book giving the
'order' of the Passover celebrations)

Box of matzah and Matzah cover
Shofar (ram's horn)
Rosh Hashanah cards
Dreidle
Torah scrolls (miniature)
Torah Yad
Chanukiyah (nine branched
candlestick)
Hannukah cards
Mezuzah
Kosher food/wine labels and packets
Menorah (candlestick)
Bar Mitzvah cards
Ketubah (wedding certificate)

Sikhism

Chauri, which is waved in front of the
Guru Granth Sahib
Romalla - the cloths that cover the
Guru Granth Sahib (when it is not in
use)
Kangha (comb)
Kachh (shorts)

Kes (turban)
Khanda (shield with Sikh symbols)
Kirpan (sword)
Kara (bangle)
Tape of Sikh music
Picture or model of the Golden
Temple at Amritsar

Books on using artefacts

Religious Artefacts in the Classroom, Gateshill and Thompson, Hodder and Stoughton
Investigating Artefacts in Religious Education - a guide for primary teachers (but useful for
secondary teachers), Howard C, RMEP
Artefacts Notes, Howard C, Articles of Faith (see below)

Obtaining artefacts

There are a number of specialist religious shops in major towns and cities which sell
religious artefacts. Some bookshops also stock a limited range. A mail order service is
available from:

Articles of Faith
Bury Business Centre
Kay Street
Bury
BL9 6BU
Tel: 0161 705 1878
Fax: 0161 763 3421

Religion in Evidence
Monk Road
Alfreton
Derbyshire
DE55 7RL
Tel: 01773 830255
Fax: 01773 830325

Both firms provide attractive catalogues which give information on a wide selection of
artefacts from the six principal religions. They sell collections of artefacts for each
faith.

Videotape suppliers

Both the BBC and ITV produce educational programmes for schools. These can be copied from the television without seeking copyright permission to use them in schools. CTVC is a company which produces videos useful for RE. Video Plus Direct can usually locate any video you might need. Film Education produces booklets and information about films which are suitable to be used in schools.

CTVC
Beeson's Yard
Bury Lane
Rickmansworth
Hertfordshire
WD3 1DS
Tel: 01923 777933
Fax: 01923 896368

Video Plus Direct
P O Box 190
Peterborough
PE2 6UW
Tel: 01733 232800
Fax: 01733 238966

Film Education
41-42 Berners Street
London
W1P 3AA

Wallcharts

Pictorial Charts Educational Trust Wallcharts Ltd
27 Kirchen Road
London
W13 0UD

Examining Boards

GCSE

Southern Examining
Group (SEG)
Stage Hill House
Guildford
Surrey
GU2 5XJ
Tel: 01483 506506
Fax: 01483 300152

Midland Examining
Group (MEG)
Syndicate Buildings
1 Hills Road
Cambridge
CB1 2EU
Tel: 01223 553311
Fax: 01223 460278

Northern Examinations
and Assessment Board
(NEAB)
Devas Street
Manchester
M15 6EX
Tel: 0161 953 1180
Fax: 0161 273 7572

Welsh Joint Education
Committee (WJEC)
245 Western Avenue
Cardiff
CF5 2YX
Tel: 01222 265000
Fax: 01222 575994

ED Excel
London Examinations
Stewart House
32 Russell Square
London
WC1B 5DN
Tel: 0171 331 4000
Fax: 0171 331 4044/45

AS and A Level

OCEAC
1 Hills Road
Cambridge
CB1 2EU
Tel: 01223 553311
Fax: 01223 460278

Northern (NEAB)
Devas Street
Manchester
M15 6EX
Tel: 0161 953 1180
Fax: 0161 273 7572

ED Excel
London Board
Stewart House
32 Russell Square
London
WC1B 5DN
Tel: 0171 331 4000
Fax: 0171 331 4044/45

Welsh Joint Education
Committee
245 Western Avenue
Cardiff
CF5 2YX
Tel: 01222 265000
Fax: 01222 575994

NI Council for the
Curriculum,
Examinations and
Assessment (CCEA)
Beechill House
42 Beechill Road
Belfast
BT8 4RS
Tel: 01232 704666
Fax: 01232 799913

Organisations

SCAA
Newcombe House
45 Notting Hill Gate
London
W11 3JB
Tel: 0171 229 1234

Culham Institute
60 East Saint Helen
Street
Abingdon
Oxfordshire
OX14 5EB
Tel: 01235 520458

SHAP Working Party
The National Society's
RE Centre
36 Causton Street
London
SW1P 4AU
Tel: 0171 932 1194

RESPECT
7 Elyham
Purley-on-Thames
Pangbourne
Berkshire
RG8 8EN
Tel: 01734 843664

CEM Christian
Education Movement
Royal Buildings
Victoria Street
Derby
DE1 1GW
Tel: 01332 296655
Fax: 01332 343253

RE-XS Religious
Education Exchange
Service
University College of
St. Martin
Lancaster
LA1 3JD
Tel: 01524 63446 Ext.
4532

The Farmington
Institute for Christian
Studies
Harris Manchester
College
Mansfield Road
Oxford
OX1 3TD
Tel: 01865 271965
Fax: 01865 271969

Independent Schools'
RS Association
c/o Harrow School
High Street,
Harrow on the Hill
Middlesex
HA1 311W
Tel: 0181 869 1225
Fax: 0181 422 6818

The Chaplains'
Encyclical
c/o Harrow School
High Street,
Harrow on the Hill
Middlesex
HA1 311W
Tel: 0181 869 1225
Fax: 0181 422 6818.

ACT Association of
Christian Teachers
94A London Road
St. Albans
Hertfordshire
AL1 1NX
Tel: 01727 840298

Catholic Education
Service
39 Eccleston Square
London
SW1V 1BX
Tel: 0171 828 7604

Free Church Federal
Council
27 Tavistock Square
London
WC1H 9HH
Tel: 0171 387 8413

Church of England
Board of Education
Church House
Great Smith Street
London
SW1P 3NZ
Tel: 0171 222 9011
Fax: 0171 233 2592

The National Society's
RE Centre
36 Causton Street
London
SW1P 4AU
Tel: 0171 932
1190/1191
Fax: 0171 932 1199

Inter-Faith Network
for the United
Kingdom
5-7 Tavistock Place
London
WC1H 9SN
Tel: 0171 388 0008
Fax: 0171 387 7968

Buddhist Society
58 Eccleston Square
London
SW1V 1PH
Tel: 0171 834 5858

British Sikh Education
Council
10 Featherstone Road
Southall
Middlesex
Tel: 0181 574 1902

Hindu Council of
Birmingham
Manor House
Office 20, 2nd Floor
40 Moat Lane
Birmingham
B5 5BD
Tel: 0121 622 6946

Muslim Educational
Trust
130 Stroud Green
Road
London
N4 3RZ
Tel: 0171 272 8502
Fax: 0171 281 3457

The Board of Deputies
of British Jews
Commonwealth House
1-19 New Oxford
Street
London
WC1A 1NF
Tel: 0171 543 5400
Fax: 0171 543 0010

Main RE centres

Westhill RE Centre
Westhill College
Selly Oak
Birmingham
B29 6LL
Tel: 0121 472 7248
Fax: 0121 415 5399

*National Society RE
Centre*
36 Causton Street
London
SW1P 4AU
Tel: 0171 932 1190
Fax: 0171 932 1199

BFSS National RE Centre
Brunel University
Osterley Campus
Isleworth
Middlesex
TW7 5DU
Tel: 0181 891 0121

York RE Centre
University College of
Ripon and York St.
John
Lord Mayors Walk
York.
YO3 7EX
Tel: 01904 616858
Fax: 01904 612512

*Welsh National Centre
for RE*
University of Wales
School of Education
Deniol Road
Bangor
Gwynedd
LL57 2UW
Tel: 01248 382761
Fax: 01248 382155

INDEX

Also by Chris Wright

Delivering Collective Worship

Now established as the leading text in this area and in use in over 1500 schools, Chris Wright's book unravels what the law and inspection teams require of collective worship in school. The main premise of the book is that it is possible to meet the legal requirements and provide a worthwhile experience for pupils without alienating colleagues, and to do this in such a way that collective worship comes to enrich the broader life of the school.

Delivering Collective Worship includes:

• advice and guidance on the use of visitors and artefacts;

• twenty ideas for stimulating and unusual school assemblies;

• a detailed bibliography of story books and assemblies.

£13.95 plus £1.25 p&p

Use a school order form or fax 01284 703300 for immediate delivery

COURSEWARE PUBLICATIONS

**4 Apple Barn Court, Westley
Bury St Edmunds, Suffolk, IP33 3TJ
Telephone & Fax: 01284 703300**